The Transcendentalist Constant
in American Literature

THE GOTHAM LIBRARY
OF THE NEW YORK UNIVERSITY PRESS

The Gotham Library is a series of original works and critical studies published in paperback primarily for student use. The Gotham hardcover edition is primarily for use by libraries and the general reader. Devoted to significant works and major authors and to literary topics of enduring importance, Gotham Library texts offer the best in literature and criticism.

Comparative and Foreign Language Literature:
  Robert J. Clements, Editor

Comparative and English Language Literature:
  James W. Tuttleton, Editor

T. W. D. Snodgrass,
in memory of Hammamet,
with my best regards,

R. A.

The Transcendentalist
Constant in
American Literature

Roger Asselineau

New York University Press · New York *and* London

Library of Congress Cataloging in Publication Data

Asselineau, Roger.
  The transcendentalist constant in American literature.
  (The Gotham library of the New York University Press)
  Includes bibliographical references and index.
    1. American literature—History and criticism—
Addresses, essays, lectures.   2. Transcendentalism
(New England)—Addresses, essays, lectures.
3. Whitman, Walt, 1819-1892—Criticism and inter-
pretation—Addresses, essays, lectures.   I. Title.
PS121.A8   810'.9'13   80-17918
ISBN 0-8147-0572-3
ISBN 0-8147-0573-1

Preface

The essays which make up this volume were written over a number of years without preconceived design, but all somehow obeyed mysterious centripetal forces and converged toward the same center, namely the ingrained idealism of American literature. Though I was unaware of it at the time, they were the result of an organic creation, as befits their subject.

They do not bear on transcendentalism proper in all its complexities and inner contradictions, but rather on transcendentalism reduced to its lowest common denominator and, as such, present in varying proportions in nearly all American authors from the birth of historical transcendentalism down to our own time. In other words, my aim has been, not a study in depth of all the implications of transcendentalism, but an attempt to isolate, or at least point to, the fundamental romanticism of American literature. Most American writers are avowed or crypto-romantics, crypto-transcendentalists, and seem to have heard Victor Hugo's injunction to poets: "This is the mysterious law: go beyond." [1] This watchword echoes Emerson's half-humorous definition of transcendentalism in his *Journal* for October 6, 1836: "Transcendentalism means, says our accomplished Mrs. B., with a wave of her hand, *a little beyond."*

Throughout this book and especially in the first chapters, the emphasis is on Whitman rather than on Emerson, though Emerson was the founding father of transcendentalism and Whitman never even was, *stricto sensu,* a transcendentalist at all. But it was Whitman who entered the Promised Land of transcendentalist poetry which Emerson was allowed to see only from afar. He succeeded better than Emerson in transmuting the disincarnate concepts of transcendentalism into poems of flesh and blood (Chapter 1), although he constantly transcended material reality in his pilgrimage from Paumanok to more than America and even to more than India (Chapter 5) toward the "secret of the earth and sky." Of the four elements, he preferred water, which, being both fluid and solid, stands halfway, as it were, between spirit and matter. In *Leaves of Grass,* his imagination liquefied rather than etherealized the world (Chapter 3). At times, when he juggled with the real world and the ideal world, he almost rivaled Paul Bunyan, and his exuberant and bombastic lyricism came close to a form of co[s]mic humor (Chapter 4). His divided allegiance to matter and spirit made him acknowledge the influence of his heredity and environment on the formation of his personality and at the same time proclaim the transcendental independence of his genius. He believed in both roots and ethereality. And, consequently, he recognized the validity of Taine's theory about race, place, and time and admitted that poets are made, but stuck nonetheless to Horace's adage that they are born (Chapter 6).

After this exploration of some aspects of Whitman's transcendentalism, a number of chapters are devoted to a few of his spiritual heirs in the twentieth century. Though at first sight Dreiser may seem to be in diametrical opposition to Whitman because he was by choice a naturalistic novelist (in fact, like Sister Carrie, he could have said: "Sister Carrie, c'est moi!"), he constantly yielded to "the lure of the spirit" and found beauty and mystery in the most banal and trivial sights. Chicago filled him with the same wonder as Walden Pond did Thoreau (Chapter 7).

Although his characters could express their wonder before a glorious sunset only by exclaiming: "How purty!" O'Neill, too, believed in the beauty and mystery of the world. He sensed invisible forces at work in things, from elms to men (Chapter 8). As for Sherwood Anderson, he was more interested in what you cannot see than in what you do see. He was always trying to make his reader feel "something" hidden behind appearances (Chapter 9). Hemingway, who was his disciple for a time, similarly attempted to suggest the submerged seven-eighths of the iceberg by carefully describing the one-eighth that everyone can see. His swashbuckling and bellicose attitudes hid a profound love of Woman, which even bloomed into love of love and a quasi-mystical love of all that exists in *The Old Man and the Sea* (Chapter 10).

Concentrating on sexual desire, but transcending it, Tennessee Williams also celebrates the power and mystery of love, even if he often shows it in a lurid and tragic light (Chapter 11). However, the most faithful disciple of Walt Whitman in our time is a poet whose work has remained largely unrecognized by critics: Walter Lowenfels, who kept up with unshaken faith the tradition of a cosmic and democratic poetry in a period of doubt and uncertainties (Chapter 12).

Notes

1. "Poètes, voilà la loi mystérieuse: allez au delà" ("Promontorium Somnii").

Contents

Acknowledgments

I am grateful to the editors under whose copyrights some of these essays originally appeared, and who granted permission to publish them here in the same or a modified version:

1. "Dreaming in the Grass," in *Forum,* vol. 14, no. 1 (Spring 1976), pp. 31-37.

2. "Walt Whitman's Humor," in *American Transcendental Quarterly,* vol. 22, part 3 (Spring 1974), pp. 86-91.

3. "Walt Whitman: From Paumanok to More than America," in *Papers on Language and Literature,* vol. 5, supplement (Summer 1969), pp. 18-39.

4. "Passage to India," in *Calamus,* no. 16 (August 1978), pp. 11-14.

5. "Whitman's Variations on Horace's Adage, or A Poet Is Both Born and Made," originally "A Poet's Dilemma: Walt Whitman's Attitude to Literary History and Literary Criticism," in Leon Edel, ed., *Literary History and Literary Criticism* (New York: New York University Press, 1964), pp. 50-61.

6. "Theodore Dreiser's Transcendentalism," in G. A. Bonnard,

ed., *English Studies Today, Second Series* (Bern: Francke Verlag, 1961), pp. 233-43.

7. *"Desire Under the Elms,* A Phase of E. O'Neill's Philosophy," in Eduard Kolb and Jörg Hasler, eds., *Festschrift Rudolf Stamm* (Bern: Francke Verlag, 1969), pp. 277-83.

1.

Dreaming in the Grass

Birds flying in the air over a river,
And children playing in a meadow beside it,
A stream that turns an ancient wheel
Under great trees.
And cattle in the water,
Below the trees.
And sun, and shade,
And warmth, and grass.
And myself
And not myself
Dreaming in the grass.[1]

Who wrote this poem? Most readers, led into error by such key words as "grass," "myself" and "not myself," will answer: "Walt Whitman!" Actually the author of this piece is Dreiser, a naturalistic writer who occasionally composed transcendentalist poetry, a Marxist whose so-called naturalistic novels often have transcendentalist overtones. It appeared in 1926 in *Moods—Cadenced and Declaimed*, a collection of poems in free verse which he kept revising and enriching through several editions, as Walt Whitman did with *Leaves of Grass*. Dreiser felt so close to the transcendentalists that in 1938 he accepted the task of editing *The Living Thoughts of Thoreau* for Longmans, Green's "Library of Living Thoughts."

Another naturalistic novelist, Jack London, was undoubtedly thinking of *Leaves of Grass* in *Martin Eden* when he made his hero confide to the girl he loves: "This grass is more beautiful to me now that I know why it is grass [he has just been studying the theory of evolution], and all the hidden chemistry of sun and rain and earth that makes it become grass. Why, there is romance in the life-history of any grass, yes, and adventure, too. The very thought of it stirs me. When I think of the play of force and matter, and all the tremendous struggle of it, I feel as if I could write an epic on the grass." [2]

Melville, too, almost felt like writing *Leaves of Grass*, even before Whitman thought of it, for, on June 1, 1851, at a time when his poems were just beginning to germinate in Whitman's mind, on a beautiful summer day similar to the "transparent summer morning" on which Whitman had the ecstasy he described in section 5 of "Song of Myself," Melville also experienced the "all" feeling and wrote to Hawthorne:

> This "all" feeling, though, there is some truth in. You must often have felt it, lying in the grass on a warm summer's day. Your legs seem to send out shoots into the earth. Your hair feels like leaves upon your head. This is the *all* feeling. But what plays mischief with the truth is that men will insist upon the universal application of a temporary feeling or opinion.[3]

Melville was too spiritually and intellectually restless to be permanently satisfied with this mood of transcendentalist optimism, but he remained faithful to grass, despite appearances, to the end of his life, for it appears again in the most despairing of all his stories, *Bartleby the Scrivener*. When Bartleby dies of existentialist disgust in the central yard of the Tombs, Melville points out: "The Egyptian character of the masonry weighed upon me with its gloom. But a soft imprisoned turf grew under foot. The heart of the eternal pyramids, it seemed, wherein by some strange magic, through the clefts, grass-seed, dropped by birds, had sprung," [4] and had thus become a sort of living hieroglyphic meaning *ankh,* eternal life and hope.

"On my volcano grows the grass," wrote Emily Dickinson, for her part, in the solitude of her house at Amherst.[5]

As for Emerson, he had been the first to meditate upon it in the Paris Jardin des Plantes in 1833, when, tired of preaching withered dogmas, he decided to shift his allegiance from theology to natural history. "Nothing is indifferent to the wise," he noted in one of his very first lectures. "If a man should study the economy of a spire of grass—how it sucks up sap, how it imbibes light, how it resists cold, how it repels excessive moisture, it would show him a design in the form, in the colour, in the smell, in the very posture of the blade as it bends before the wind . . . the whole of Nature is a metaphor or image of the human mind." [6]

Whitman's grass thus grows all over American literature both before and after him. It crops up in the most unexpected places, from Melville's correspondence to Dreiser's *Moods,* from Emily Dickinson's poems to Jack London's adventure stories. It is to be found even in contemporary literature. Though Dos Passos's *USA* seems an unpromising place for it, it is mentioned in the very first "Camera Eye" section, where the author describes himself as a child walking along a street in a Belgian city before World War I, stepping carefully "so as not to step on the bright anxious grass-blades . . . but walking fast you have to tread on too many grass-blades the poor hurt green tongues shrink under your feet. . . ." [7] This grass reappears stubbornly—in an ethereal form—at the end of the trilogy when Vag "waits at the end of the concrete . . . at the edge of the hissing speeding string of cars where the reek of ether and gas melts into the silent grassy smell of the earth." [8] Two world wars later, in the "Introduction" to his *Midpoint and Other Poems,* John Updike, the chronicler, of suburbia, declared his intention of singing "the sweet cold grass that had no name," killed by the weed-killers of the suburbanites, but eternal for all their efforts, and concluded: "death has no other name than *ankh,* life." [9] He seems to have been unaffected by the "dissociation of sensibility" of which T. S. Eliot complained. His imagination is omnivorous, feeds on and digests everything from scientific laws to the most sordid details of everyday life, for all things are meaningful to him:

> The beaded curtain
> of Matter hid[es] an understanding Eye . . .[10]

and

> . . . throughout phenomena
> Flashes the sword of Universal Law.[11]

Robert Duncan, who, from the start, believed in "Roots and Branches," [12] turns his back on the Dance of Death of the Dark Ages, and prefers to dance the Dance of Life. He celebrates it in a poem called "The Dance," in the course of which he joins hands with Whitman:

> Whitman was right. Our names are left
>   like leaves of grass,
> likeness and liking, the human greenness,
>
> tough as grass that survives cruelest seasons.[13]

Ronald Johnson, a poet of the next generation, in the *Valley of the Many-colored Grasses* (1969) wrote "letters to Walt Whitman" about

> the great grassy world
> that surrounds us
>   singing.

He too has "plucked a stalk of grass" from Walt Whitman's "ample prairie." [14]

Irving Feldman, singing the song of "Is" in *Leaping Clear* (1976), celebrates the miraculous synthesis of sunlight, water, and earth called grass:

and grass comes up
singulars out of the earth
lifting their spears and shouting *Ahhhh!* [15]

Sylvia Plath observed its tenacious growth through the stones of cities:

The city waits and aches. The little grasses
Crack through stone, and they are green with life.[16]

As for Tennessee Williams, he sometimes dreams nostalgically of the essential grass which he trod before trailing clouds of glory here below, the "heavenly grass" in which he used to walk before his "feet came down to walk on earth." [17] He believes in the irresistible strength of grass in general and violets in particular. In *Camino Real,* he points out that "The violets in the mountains can break the rocks, if you believe in them and allow them to grow!" [18] W. C. Williams has the same faith in saxifrage: ". . . saxifrage is my flower, that splits the rocks." [19]

This omnipresence of grass is not accidental. It corresponds to an essential characteristic and a specific trait of American literature which distinguishes it radically from all other western literatures: its transcendentalist quality. Transcendentalism, far from being a dead and irrelevant philosophy confined to the first half of the nineteenth century, is a fertilizing undercurrent, a constant in American literature from Emerson down to our own time, though it appeared under quite different circumstances when the United States was primarily agrarian, and industry and social problems hardly existed. One of the implications of this permanence is that most American novelists are essentially poets, who write romances rather than true novels. They believe in insights rather than ideas, in intuitions rather than cold reason. They are "failed poets," as Faulkner once said of himself—whereas European novelists, to the exclusion perhaps of their British colleagues—often are intellectuals and even, sometimes, especially in France, professional philosophers.

The first quality required of a poet is a keen sense of wonder. Now most American writers are richly endowed with it. They "see the miraculous in the common" like Emerson.[20] They loaf and invite their souls like Whitman, and like him "sing the commonplace" [21] and feel that "every hour of the light and dark is a miracle." [22] They practice "a true sauntering of the eye" like Thoreau: "What I need," he said, "is not to look at all, but a true sauntering of the eye," [23] an eye which no film of custom has covered yet, so that it can see the sun, which most people have gone blind to, as Emerson pointed out. American writers do see it, and discover the world anew every morning. They see without looking, as it were, whereas nonromantic European writers perhaps look without seeing. They are literally intoxicated with sensations and draw up ecstatic inventories of the world which at times tend to become interminable—as when Whitman, after absorbing the Kosmos, regurgitates it in his endless catalogues, or Thomas Wolfe takes mental snapshots of everything he sees without omitting a detail. Theirs is a deeply religious attitude toward things. They perceive the world through all their senses and worship it. They could all echo Wordsworth's "To me the meanest flower that blows can give / Thoughts that do often lie too deep for tears." [24] For them as for Whitman, "a curl of smoke or a hair on the back of [one of their] hands" is "just as curious as any revelation." [25] This is true of most American storytellers. They are less interested in telling stories than in recording revelations, epiphanies. Sherwood Anderson's short stories in particular are hardly stories at all. Very often nothing happens in them. They begin nowhere and end nowhere. They merely express his wonder before "odd little things," [26] as he calls them, which transfix him to the ground. He gives a striking example of it in *A Story Teller's Story* when he tells how once "a man and a woman [having a little domestic flare-up] in a garden had become [to him] the center of a universe about which it seemed [he] might think and feel in joy and wonder forever." [27] His characters are no ordinary men and women. Some of them are poets like Dr. Reefy in *Winesburg, Ohio.* They see beyond mere appearances; they are in touch with the central reality of the universe like Joe Welling, who had discovered that decay is fire, that everything is burning up and "the world is on fire." [28]

Even Hemingway, who is supposed to be a man of action, writing about other men of action, is less concerned with events than with impressions—especially in his short stories. "Big Two-Hearted River" suggests internal rather than external space, "l'espace du dedans," as Henri Michaux, the Belgian poet, calls it. The "action" takes place in the hero's consciousness rather than in the outer world. It concerns a spiritual rather than a physical experience; and this would not be such a bad description of some of Hemingway's longer books, of *Death in the Afternoon,* and *Green Hills of Africa* especially, where he captures our attention not by skillfully creating suspense, but by enlisting us in his quest of some elusive truth (the meaning of life and death). The animals he was so stubbornly chasing in Kenya were in fact closer to legendary unicorns than to actual kudus.

Thoreau spent nearly all his life traveling in Concord. In this as in other respects he was—at least in appearance—an exception. American writers in general need a broader field of investigation and constantly roam the world in search of new sights and sounds, either in imagination like Whitman, who sang his "Song of the Open Road" without leaving New York, or in person, like Jack Kerouac and his Dharma Bums. Yet they look rather backward than forward, and, for all their craving for Experience, always think nostalgically of their lost childish Innocence. Like Huckleberry Finn they dream of "lighting out" for some distant territory, where no grown-ups will ever interfere with their activities. Thus in due time Holden Caulfield succeeds Huck, but finds out that his escape route has been cut off by civilization and the closing of the frontier. They all instinctively believe that "the child is father of the man," and trails after him "clouds of glory." They miss "the visionary gleam," "the glory and the dream." [29] Though Nick Adams grows older from one novel to another, he reappears as young and boyish as ever under the name of Manolin by the side of old Santiago in *The Old Man and the Sea,* and the Old Man himself is still a child at heart and dreams of lions playing like young cats on the white beaches of Africa in a prelapsarian world where nothing has to kill in order to survive. Even Julien Green, who has written all his books in French, is a transcendentalist at heart, who, as a French critic pointed out, "rare aventure en France, a toujours gardé 'The Age of Innocence.' " [30]

Children, who hardly ever appeared in literature before romanticism, except to get murdered in Elizabethan dramas, crop up again and again in American literature, either as good bad boys (Peck's Bad Boy and Tom Sawyer), or as fundamentally good boys lost in a world of drunks, murderers, crooks, negro-haters and phoneys of all kinds (Huck Finn, Holden Caulfield, and the boy-hero of *Other Voices, Other Rooms,* or even Holly Golightly in *Breakfast at Tiffany's,* since with Truman Capote, the sex does not matter much). They are not only better than their elders, but also infinitely wiser. "The first questions are always to be asked and the wisest doctor is graveled by the inquisitiveness of the child," Emerson had already noted.[31] The inquisitive child tirelessly asking the same naïve and yet disconcerting questions turns up in "Song of Myself" and asks the poet "what is the grass?" and *Leaves of Grass,* and in a way all subsequent American literature, are attempts to answer this most difficult question in a more or less "indirect" or circuitous manner.

In order to do so and not get lost in the great cosmic chaos or void of the world, American writers adopt the same strategy as Emerson's child; they cling to small details, they keep "individualizing everything, generalizing nothing." [32] Hemingway, for his part, after going through the ordeal of World War I, discovered that "There were many words that you could not stand to hear and finally only the names of places had dignity. . . . Abstract words such as glory, honor, courage or hallow were obscene beside the concrete names of villages, the numbers of roads, the names of rivers, the numbers of regiments and the dates." [33] And that was one of the reasons he needed the order and clarity of a "clean well-lighted place" and wrote with such sharpness and precision. In this respect, American poets distil a poetry which is often strikingly different from the poetry written theoretically in the same language by their counterparts in England. English poets live in a world of blurred outlines, while American poets inhabit a world of solid objects with sharp edges and well-defined shapes and enjoy it. "The greatest poverty is not to live in a physical world," [34] Wallace Stevens declared; and Marianne Moore loved to describe things with myopic accuracy—a Gloria Mundi camellia, for instance:

> . . . a leaf two inches nine lines broad they have; and the
>   smaller Camellia Sabina

> with amanita-white petals; there are several of her pale
> pin-wheels, and pale stripe that looks as if on a mushroom
> the sliver from a beetroot carved were laid [35]

Looking at a rose, she does not miss that frequently overlooked
detail: the thorn. "Your thorns are the best part of you," she per-
versely concludes in "Roses Only." [36] As for Gertrude Stein, she
stubbornly repeated: "Rose is a rose is a rose is a rose," [37] which
Hemingway echoed in a lower key: "An onion is an onion, is an
onion," [38] while W. B. Yeats, preferring essences to mere existences,
sang "the rose of all roses," the "rose of all the World." [39]

The physical world is thus fully rehabilitated in American literature and small details regarded as infinitely precious. As Emerson
said, "the day of facts is a rock of diamonds." [40] Thoreau also
believed it, but specified that "it is wholesomer to look at the
ground much than at the heavens," [41] for "Heaven is under our
feet as well as over our heads." [42] Hemingway admired him for this
belief and imitated his terseness and unemotional approach. Most
American writers, like him, prefer solid objects to vague emotions,
or treat objects as "objective correlatives." T. S. Eliot coined the
phrase, but did not invent the thing.

And yet, though in American literature minute particulars are
rendered with striking accuracy and admirable immediacy (when
Hemingway's characters drink *grappa* or *vino rosso,* the reader feels
thirsty; when one of them punches his opponent, the reader is hit
full in the face), they are never wrenched from their cosmic context. They are both hard matter which one cannot put one's foot
through (Thoreau's test) and ethereal spirit. This is one of the
contradictions which make transcendentalism so fecund and dynamic, so "electric," one of Whitman's favorite words. The contradictory elements (idealism versus materialism, individualism
versus democracy, etc.) which make it up can be compared to
electrodes of opposite signs which produce dazzling flashes as soon
as they are brought into contact with each other. They create vital
tensions.

For Emerson, "a leaf [of grass presumably], a drop, a crystal, a
moment of time is related to the whole and partakes of the perfection of the whole." [43] "They are but parts, anything is but a
part," [44] Whitman added, and like Wordsworth saw "the parts as

parts, but with a feeling of the whole." [45] Most American writers have, like the transcendentalists, a vivid sense of the infinity of space and time, which they probably owe to the infinite spaces of the American continent, to that intense feeling of *Geworfensein* or isolation which I have too summarily analyzed elsewhere under the name of "Ishmael complex." [46] American novelists are thus less concerned with man in society than with "man against the sky." [47] Like Walt Whitman's "noiseless patient spider," they feel lost in the middle of a great vacant space, in "a clean well-lighted place" surrounded with nada on all sides, "in measureless oceans of space." But, instead of taking refuge in a cluttered Victorian drawing room in some crowded European capital as Henry James did, each of them weaves his web where he happens to be. Suspended in the void, "ceaselessly musing, venturing, throwing," he "launch[es] forth filament, filament, filament, out of [himself]" till he has covered with the cobweb of his works the great existential void which originally surrounded him. In other words, each of them fills the great open spaces of the American continent with his own substance, with himself, with his dreams. He becomes one with America in the middle of his cobweb. So all the books of the American writer are "Songs of Myself" as well as "Songs of America." Whatever their subjects, American writers, from Mark Twain to Saul Bellow, are all Narcissuses looking at their own changing reflections in the Walden Ponds of their minds. They watch—with a good deal of complacency—their successive avatars: Mark Twain becomes in turn Huckleberry Finn, the Connecticut Yankee at King Arthur's Court, and even Joan of Arc, whereas Saul Bellow remains fundamentally the same "dangling man" in all his novels. They all think they are describing the physical world while they are merely expressing themselves, adding to the world "the gleam / The light that never was on sea or land, / The consecration and the Poet's dream." [48] Anyway, thanks to their "esemplastic power," [49] i.e., their power of shaping things into one, they see the whole and perceive the design of the mosaic, while most of us, being short-sighted, see only a few meaningless, colored stones under our noses.

One of the reasons for the unremitting interest of American writers in the outside world is that they always see it (more or less consciously) as made up of hieroglyphics to be deciphered, of "illustrious [or trivial] Providences" to be recorded and interpreted. They all rewrite *Magnalia Christi Americana* in their own style, since, as Emerson said, "the visible creation is the terminus, or the circumference of the invisible. . . . Facts which had never before left their stark common sense, suddenly figure Eleusinian mysteries. My boots [one immediately thinks of Van Gogh's paintings] and chair and candlestick are fairies in disguise, meteors and constellations." [50] To them the meanest spider that weaves can give thoughts that do often lie too deep for tears, from Whitman's patient noiseless one to Robert Frost's dimpled, fat, and white murderer of the innocent moth on the blue heal-all. Sights lead to insights, facts become symbols. Hands in *Winesburg, Ohio,* undergo a whole series of strange metamorphoses, from piston rods to "the wings of an imprisoned bird" and "fluttering pennants of promise." Surface resemblances do not count in Sherwood Anderson's internal world. He tries to evoke the hidden life of people by painting the outside of things. With a different technique and more self-control, Hemingway often gives a mystical fifth dimension to his world of unsouled men and women and eventually re-souls them, so to speak. After all, "nada" is just another word for God, and Pascal himself was sometimes frightened by "the eternal silence of infinite space" [51] (his own definition of "nada"). All American fiction is similarly symbolical and has provided innumerable critics with inexhaustible happy hunting grounds.

Even Jewish writers born outside the transcendentalist tradition have rallied to it. The Bellovian hero is a combination of the Wandering Jew and the American Scholar. He loafs and invites his soul, and Saul Bellow himself has never hidden his debt to Whitman.[51] Malamud, for his part, seems to have chosen Thoreau as a transcendentalist forefather. One of *Dubin's Lives* is a *Life of Thoreau,* and Dubin, we are told, is "stalled by the miraculous creation and interwoven whole," and lets nature teach him and "bring forth the self he sought." [53] As for Norman Mailer, his first published book, *The Naked and the Dead* (1949), supposedly a war novel, actually describes a mystic quest with Mount Anaka in the rôle of Moby-Dick.

This American way of "seeing" has led to a new American way

of "saying." For, like Montaigne's, Emerson's words bleed when you cut them. He believed in the simple, precise concreteness of the language spoken by "strong-natured farmers and backwoodsmen," and even went so far as to claim that the language of the writer "must embrace words and images excluded from polite conversation." [54] He did not practice what he preached in this respect, but his followers have all tended to prefer the vernacular to the polished language of the well-read person, the "vulgate," as H. L. Mencken called it, to literary English. Mark Twain showed the way. Sherwood Anderson and Hemingway, among others, followed suit and opened up new possibilities of development by separating the vernacular from the childish, illiterate narrator. They gradually evolved their own version of stylized American speech, based on the accumulation and juxtaposition of isolated, unconnected concrete elements without syntactic complexities—the great leveling democracy of the "and," as Joseph Warren Beach called it.[55] Through this process the world becomes a succession of intensely perceived nows, but each of these nows has an eternal value and implies the whole of space and time. Or, to take up Hemingway's own metaphor, only one-eighth of the iceberg is visible above the surface, but it moves with such majestic slowness and power that it is impossible not to feel the presence under the water of the submerged seven eighths.[56]

Thanks to this gradual application of transcendentalist principles, American literature has acquired a voice and a language of its own, characterized by an apparently inexhaustible dynamism and a vigorous raciness. Whitman's dream has come true:

> To find a new unthought-of nonchalance with the best
>   of Nature!
> To have the gag removed from one's mouth.[57]

The exuberance consequent on this liberation sometimes results in a strange mixture of comic and cosmic elements, as Richard Chace has shown in his analyses of *Leaves of Grass*.[58] But this explosive vitality so far has prevented American literature from reaching the cul-de-sac of noncommunication and impotence in which other western literatures have eventually ended up. It is hard to imagine Norman Mailer waiting for Godot or playing an "Endgame."

It may be objected, however, that in their search for innocence and spontaneity American writers have always tended to despise art, which they equate with artifice. True, in so doing they have liberated verse from its traditional shackles, but they have also too often preferred formlessness to form and triteness to "style." In this respect, O'Neill was probably the worst offender of them all—a great tragic writer and a tragic failure as an artist with only "a touch of the poet."

Mark Twain said: ". . . there is not a single human characteristic which can safely be labeled as American." [59] This is quite true. Yet, American literature can safely be labeled American, thanks to the presence in it of the peculiar transcendentalist ingredient which our analyses have detected. The American transcendentalist, by carrying the romantic revolution further than the Europeans, and by developing its implications more consistently than the writers of any western literature, created something new which has enabled their successors to build a national literature independent of English literature, even though in principle they used the same language. It is thanks to this bunch of New England eccentrics that American literature acquired as early as the beginning of the nineteenth century a distinctive personality, an unmistakable tone of its own which it has kept ever since.

This now obvious, now hidden and elusive transcendentalist factor seems to be the main source of its charm and power as well as some of its limitations, for its emphasis on innocence often condemns it to a certain immaturity and also to a regrettable tendency to regard inarticulateness as the best proof of sincerity. Moreover, making naïveté the gauge of feeling easily leads to sentimentality, superficiality, and diffuseness. The spirit killeth the letter. It is perhaps because of the existence of this transcendentalist undercurrent that American literature has too often shown itself suspicious of the analytical intellect ("there are no ideas but in things," according to William Carlos Williams) and indifferent to harmonious structures, too reluctant to develop a "nuancé" reaction to society and too hungry for vague metaphysical speculations. But these are only the defects of its qualities, and we must be grateful to transcendentalism for breathing into American literature a passionate and unremitting interest in concrete reality, a reverent love of all things, as well as a vitality, a freshness and vigor which have but rarely been attained by other literatures.

Notes

1. Theodore Dreiser, "Proteus," *Moods Cadenced and Declaimed* (New York: Boni & Liveright, 1926), p. 7.
2. Jack London, *Martin Eden* (New York: Jack London Society, 1936), p. 111. See Roger Asselineau, "Jack London et Walt Whitman." *Europe*, vol. 54, p. 76 (Jan.-Feb. 1976).
3. *Portable Melville* (New York: Viking Press, 1952), p. 434.
4. Ibid., p. 511.
5. Poem no. 1677 in *The Complete Poems of Emily Dickinson*, ed. by Thomas H. Johnson (Boston: Little, Brown, 1960), p. 685.
6. *Early Lectures*, vol. I, p. 17.
7. John Dos Passos, *U.S.A.* (New York: Modern Library [1939]), p. 5.
8. Ibid., p. 559.
9. John Updike, *Midpoint and Other Poems* (New York: Fawcett, 1970), pp. 3, 62.
10. Ibid., "Introduction," p. 5.
11. Ibid., "Conclusion," p. 39.
12. This is the title of his first collection of poems, published by Scribner's in 1964.
13. Donald M. Allen, ed., *The New American Poetry, 1945-1960* (New York: Grove Press, 1960), p. 46. "The Dance" is dated 1956.
14. Quoted in Hayden Carruth, ed., *The Voice That Is Great Within Us* (New York: Bantam Books, 1970), pp. 701-2.
15. *Leaping Clear* (New York: Viking Pess, 1976), p. 10.
16. *Winter Trees* (New York: Harper & Row, 1972), p. 52.
17. "Heavenly Grass," *In The Winter of Cities* (Norfolk, Conn.: New Directions, 1956), p. 97.
18. *Camino Real* (Norfolk, Conn.: New Directions, 1953), p. 97.
19. "A Sort of Song," *Collected Later Poems* (Norfolk, Conn.: New Directions, 1963), p. 7.
20. Ralph Waldo Emerson, "Prospects," *Complete Works* (Boston: Houghton Mifflin, 1903), vol. I, p. 78.
21. Walt Whitman, "The Commonplace," l. 1, *Leaves of Grass* (New York: W. W. Norton, 1973), p. 553.
22. Ibid., l. 17, p. 389.
23. Henry David Thoreau, *Complete Works* (Boston: Houghton Mifflin, 1906), vol. X, p. 351.

24. William Wordsworth, "Ode on Intimations of Immortality," ll. 206-207, *The Poetical Works* (London: Oxford University Press, 1913), p. 590 B.

25. Walt Whitman, "Song of Myself," sec. 41, l. 1039 (New York: W. W. Norton, 1973), p. 75.

26. "The Man Who Became a Woman" *(Horses and Men,* 1924), in *Sherwood Anderson Reader,* ed. by Paul Rosenfeld (Boston: Houghton Mifflin, 1947), p. 148.

27. Sherwood Anderson, *A Story Teller's Story,* Bk. III, n. 4 (New York: Grove Press, 1951), p. 317.

28. Sherwood Anderson, "A Man of Many Ideas," *Winesburg, Ohio* (New York: Penguin Books, 1946), p. 69. Even a second- or third-rate writer like Zona Gale entertained a transcendentalist conception of art: "He [the artist] is a channel for the birth of beauty into our medium. He becomes so by some special grace of seeing; by that which is the beginning of all wisdom; by a heightening of perception akin to the experience which the East knows as illumination; a breaking through to another level of being to which the race shall in time come as to its own inheritance. Meanwhile the artist is the reporter of that other plane." "Beauty and the Commonplace," *Portage, Wisconsin, and Other Essays* (New York: Alfred A. Knopf, 1928), p. 167.

29. William Wordsworth, "Ode on Intimations of Immortality," Epigraph and ll. 56, 57, 64, *The Poetical Works* (London: Oxford: University Press, 1913), pp. 587-88.

30. Robert de Saint Jean, *Figaro Littéraire* (February 22, 1971), 10 C.

31. Ralph Waldo Emerson, "Intellect," *Complete Works* (Boston: Houghton Mifflin, 1903), vol. II, p. 303.

32. Ibid., vol. III, p. 185.

33. Ernest Hemingway, *A Farewell to Arms,* chap. 27 (London: Albatross Ed., 1947), p. 152.

34. Wallace Stevens, "Esthétique du mal," vol. XV, ll. 1-2, *Collected Poems* (London: Faber & Faber, 1955), p. 325.

35. Marianne Moore, "Camellia Sabina," *Collected Poems* (New York: Macmillan, 1961), p. 22.

36. Marianne Moore, "Roses Only," *Collected Poems* (New York: Macmillan, 1961).

37. Gertrude Stein, "Sacred Emily," in *Geography and Plays* (New York: Haskell House, 1967), p. 187.

38. Ernest Hemingway, *For Whom the Bell Tolls,* chap. 24 (London: Jonathan Cape, 1952), p. 274.

39. W. B. Yeats, "The Rose of Battles," *Collected Poems* (London: Macmillan, 1950), p. 42.

40. Quoted by F. O. Matthiessen, *American Renaissance* (New York: Oxford University Press, 1941), p. 58.

41. Henry David Thoreau, *Complete Works* (Boston: Houghton Mifflin, 1906), vol. XVI, p. 125.

42. Ibid., vol. II, p. 313.

43. Ralph Waldo Emerson, "Discipline," *Complete Works* (Boston: Houghton Mifflin, 1903), vol. I, p. 48.
44. Walt Whitman, "Song of Myself," sec. 45, l. 1195, *Leaves of Grass* (New York: W. W. Norton, 1973), p. 82.
45. William Wordsworth, *The Prelude* (version of 1805), Bk. VII, ll. 711-12 (London: Oxford University Press, 1933), p. 124.
46. Roger Asselineau, "Ishmael—or the Theme of Solitude in American Literature," *USA in Focus* (Oslo: Universitetsforlaget, 1966), pp. 107-19.
47. Title of a book of poems by Edwin Arlington Robinson: *The Man Against the Sky* (New York: Macmillan, 1916).
48. William Wordsworth, "Peele Castle," ll. 14-16, *The Poetical Works* (London: Oxford University Press, 1913), p. 578.
49. Samuel Taylor Coleridge, *Biographia Literaria,* chap. 13 (London: Dent's Everyman's Library, 1930), p. 153.
50. Ralph Waldo Emerson, "Beauty," *The Conduct of Life* (London: Macmillan, 1895), p. 247.
51. "Le silence éternel de ces espaces infinis m'effraie." Blaise Pascal, *Pensées,* ed. by Léon Brunschvig (Paris: Hachette, 1910), vol. III, item 206, p. 428.
52. See his "Distractions of a Fiction Writer," reprinted in the Viking Critical Edition of *Herzog,* ed. by Irving Howe (New York: Viking, 1976), pp. 376-79.
53. *Dubin's Lives* (London: Chatto & Windus, 1979), p. 10.
54. Quoted by F. O. Matthiessen, op. cit., p. 35.
55. Joseph Warren Beach, *American Fiction, 1920-1940* (New York: Macmillan, 1941), p. 114.
56. "The Art of Fiction—An Interview with E. Hemingway," *Paris Review,* no. 18 (Spring 1958), p. 84—reprinted in *Writers at Work,* 2nd Series (London: Secker & Warburg, 1963), p. 198.
57. Walt Whitman, "One Hour to Madness and Joy," ll. 13-14, *Leaves of Grass* (New York: W. W. Norton, 1973), p. 116.
58. *Walt Whitman Reconsidered* (New York: William Sloane, 1955).
59. Quoted by Clifton Fadiman in *The American Treasury* (New York: Harper, 1955), p. 26.

2.

Whitman, the Transcendentalist Poet Incarnate

In his lifetime, Walt Whitman was either lauded to the skies as the equal of Homer and Shakespeare or reviled as the author of obscene poems written in a medium which was neither prose nor verse. Nowadays he is universally considered the greatest American poet. Social taboos and literary conventions being no longer respected, no one who reads *Leaves of Grass* can fail to feel the power and directness of these extraordinary poems. Here is almost pure lyricism, poetry laid bare, stripped of its traditional trappings, reduced to itself, singing the self and the world without padding. Giovanni Papini, an Italian writer accustomed to entirely different forms of literature, felt this very acutely: "I must confess that *I*, a Tuscan, an Italian, a Latin, have not felt what poetry really was through Vergil or Dante—and still less through Petrarch or Tasso, luxury poets and consequently men of letters rather than poets— but, on the contrary, through the childish enumerations and impassioned evocations of the kindly harvester of *Leaves of Grass.*" Any

17

reader of Whitman can adapt this statement to his or her own culture.

I

Though a "pure" poet with a universal appeal, Whitman is also specifically an American poet. He was a kind of Quaker poet, to begin with, believing in the "inner light"; he wore his hat as he pleased indoors or out, and scrupulously avoided calling the days and months by their old pagan names. He was also like his father, a radical, an admirer of Thomas Paine, a hater of kings and priests, a believer in progress, a sympathizer with the rebels and revolutionists of all lands—a true democrat, in short, with a deeply ingrained faith in the possibility of earthly happiness for all men in conformity with the preamble to the Bill of Rights. He was a transcendentalist, too. And that is why Emerson greeted *Leaves of Grass* with such enthusiasm in 1855. It seemed to him that Whitman was the poet whose coming he had prophesied. Indeed, in many respects, *Leaves of Grass* was a translation into verse of the main tenets of the transcendentalist doctrine, and fully exploited the "yet unsung" American materials, industry included, as Emerson recommended. Emerson could even detect in it the influence of the Oriental scriptures, which he had been subject to himself, and that of the German idealists, as well. For Whitman, far from being the "rough" he claimed to be in 1855, was, on the contrary, very well read and knew in particular Hedge's *Prose Writers of Germany* and Gostwick's *German Literature*.

Thus *Leaves of Grass* was not created from nothing. One can detect in it elements anterior to its appearance and common to all transcendentalists. This, however, does not detract from its originality. Whitman borrowed liberally, but assimilated his borrowings and turned them into something new, because he had something new to express as well as a new mode of expression at his disposal.

Whitman himself was quite aware of the complexity and apparent lack of logical cohesion of his book. He declared somewhat defiantly:

> Do I contradict myself?
> Very well then I contradict myself.
> (I am large, I contain multitudes.) [1]

By this he did not refer to a static juxtaposition of contradictory elements, but rather to the presence in *Leaves of Grass* of divergent tendencies and clashing ideas. In short, his contradictions are dynamic, or, to use one of his favorite words, "electric." Like electrodes of opposite signs, they produce dazzling flashes as soon as they are brought into contact with each other. They express violent inner tensions, torturing hesitations, and passionate gropings after an everlasting but elusive truth, and they confer on his poetry its vital quality, its stimulating power. Whitman never provides us with ready-made answers, but instead invites us to follow him in his quest and even to go beyond him if we can.

One of the objects of his quest is his Self. "One's Self I sing, a simple separate person," he tells us in the very first line of *Leaves of Grass,* and that is why he eventually entitled his longest poem "Song of Myself." "Camerado," he warns us in "So Long!" this is not a book, / Who touches this, touches a man." It is true. We have no sooner opened the book than he starts singing himself and celebrating himself and presenting us with his full-length portrait:

> Walt Whitman, an American, one of the roughs, a Kosmos,
> Disorderly, fleshy and sensual . . . eating drinking and
>   breeding,
> No sentimentalist . . . . no stander above men and women or
>   apart from them . . . . No more modest than immodest.

It is clear that he wants first to give an impression of physical vigor. He tries to impose on us the image of a laborer, solidly built, proud of his strength and his carnal appetites, whose sensual instincts are not paralyzed by any inhibition. He is no "gentleman," distant and reserved. He gives free rein to his emotions and, above all, he refuses to stand apart from other people and makes common cause with all the oppressed. No social barrier stops him: "To the drudge or emptier of privies I lean . . . on his right cheek I put the family kiss," he claims. Besides, if we are to believe him, he is no intellectual, either. He exalts life in the open air, avoids libraries, and prefers the rude, bronzed, and bearded face of the vagabond always on the go to the smooth-shaven face of the city man.

Such is the portrait of the artist as a "rough" which emerges from *Leaves of Grass,* his "Me Myself," as he says. However, a more attentive reading of "Song of Myself" reveals strange dissonances. To begin with, there is the admission that he had not always possessed the faith which inspires his exultant optimism:

> Down-hearted doubters, dull and excluded
> Frivolous sullen moping angry affected disheartened
>   atheistical
> I know every one of you, and I know the unspoken
>   interrogatories,
> By experience I know them. . . .

So his exuberance concealed agonies and doubts. He was not merely the happy extrovert of his portrait. His personality was in fact far less simple than may appear at first sight. As soon as he stops talking directly about himself, the hearty superficial man of the people of the self-portrait gives way to a dreamy introverted poet:

> Apart from the pulling and hauling stands what I am,
> Stands amused, complacent, compassionating, idle, unitary,
> Looks down, is erect, bends an arm on an impalpable certain
>   rest,
> Looks with its sidecurved head curious what will come next,
> Both in and out of the game, and watching and wondering
>   at it.

He even expresses at times a deep-seated despair, as in the 1860 poem later entitled "Out of the Cradle Endlessly Rocking":

> O a word! O what is my destination?
> O I fear it is henceforth chaos!

> O how joys, dreads, convolutions, human shapes and all
>   shapes, spring as from graves around me!

Clearly, there were discordant elements at the heart of his exuberant optimism. The jolly fellow of the official portrait was actually very unstable, passing back and forth between exaltation and gloom. Whitman himself compared his life to a long sea voyage during which the ship seemed several times about to sink. He exaggerated hardly at all. Each new edition of *Leaves of Grass* marked the victorious outcome of a spiritual crisis. He was lacerated by doubts caused by the universal presence of evil, tortured by what he considered shameful desires, but his art saved him by permitting him to express (in the etymological meaning of the word) the turbulent passions which possessed him. (In this sense, *Leaves of Grass* is like Baudelaire's poems, *Flowers of Evil.*) It preserved him from despair, like the solitary thrush of his poem, who

> Sings by himself a song
> Song of the bleeding throat
> Death's outlet song of life (for well dear brother I know
> If thou wast not granted to sing thou wouldst surely die.)

Thus, when we touch *Leaves of Grass,* we do touch a man, but he is not the stalwart worker and boisterous prophet Whitman thought he had put into it. He is a much more interesting man, whom we might call "Whitman Agonistes," the adjective which Milton applied to Samson (Whitman liked it), or "Whitman the athlete" (he was fond of this word too); he was indeed the moral athlete who throughout his life victoriously fought against despair. This, however, did not mean that he was deliberately trying to deceive his readers when he depicted himself as an uneducated but inspired carpenter. For, when he did so, he was merely describing the mythical being he wished to be, rather than the man he really was. He did want to look like a common worker, since he decided about 1850 to change his way of life and renounce the world (of journalism) with all its pomp and circumstance. That he chose poverty is proof enough of his sincerity. He really dreamed of himself as the prophet of a new evangel. It was as such that he portrayed himself, and henceforward he tried to resemble his own portrait and identified himself completely with his book. There is not the least justification therefore for accusing him of assuming a pose, as has sometimes been done.

Though the Self looms large in the book and "Song of Myself" towers above all the other poems, the whole volume is nonetheless impersonally entitled *Leaves of Grass.* This is an unusual phrase, but Whitman preferred it to "blades of grass." In his eyes, it symbolized the universality and eternity of "Life":

> I guess it is a uniform hieroglyphic,
> And it means, Sprouting alike in broad zones and in narrow
>   zones,
> And now it seems to me the beautiful uncut hair of
>   graves. . . .
> The smallest sprout shows there is really no death. . . .

Thus, according to him, the same irresistible current of life flows through the whole cosmos, through the smallest and humblest herbaceous plants, through the animals which feed upon them, and once more through the anonymous grass which grows on their corpses when they die. Whitman constantly perceives the presence of this current behind the inert appearances of material things and translates it into poetry. He translates the leaves of universal grass into the leaves of his own book, or *Leaves of Grass,* which consequently is not a mere book, but a cluster of living presences. This all-pervading vitalism made Whitman intuitively apprehend the theory of evolution several years before Darwin formulated it in scientific terms in *The Origin of Species* (1859):

> I find I incorporate gneiss, coal, long-threaded moss, fruits,
>   grains, esculent roots,
> And am stucco'd with quadrupeds all over,
> And have distanced what is behind me with good reasons,
> Immense have been the preparations for me . . .

> My embryo has never been torpid, nothing could over-
> lay it . . .
> Vast vegetables gave it sustenance,
> Monstrous sauroids transported it in their mouths and
> deposited it with care.

For Whitman, God was essentially Life, an irresistible and indestructible force pulsing through the universe, immanent even in
apparently inanimate materials. In *Leaves of Grass,* All is God and
God is All, and this divine presence in all things confers an infinite
value even on the commonest and cheapest objects, since they are
parts of the sacred Whole. "They are but parts, anything is but a
part." Consequently, "limits, boundaries, outlines are meaningless," and Whitman can exclaim in "Song of Myself": "[I] am not
contain'd between my hat and boots." Space and Time are mere
illusions—as the German idealists had taught him—and therefore a
man exists not only where his body is, but all over the universe,
and not only in the present, but in all times:

> Space and Time! now I know what I guess'd at . . .
> My ties and ballasts leave me, I travel, I sail, my elbows rest
> in sea-gaps,
> I skirt sierras, my palms cover continents,
> I am afoot with my vision.

Whitman's was a very unorthodox position: he did not believe in a
God distinct from his creation or in the divinity of Christ. For him,
as for Elias Hicks, the Quaker heretic whom he admired, Christ
was only the latest of the prophets. Like Volney, whose *Ruins* he
had read in his youth, he thought that religions have only a relative value, and he put, in the same "portfolio," "Manito loose,
Allah on a leaf, the crucifix engraved, / With Odin and the hid-
eous-faced Mexitli and every idol and image." He wanted to found
a new religion enclosing and transcending all the others:

> My faith is the greatest of faiths and the least of faiths,
> Enclosing worship ancient and modern and all between
> ancient and modern. . . .

An original tenet of his faith was that, far from proclaiming the superiority of spirit over matter, he exalted the sacred character of the latter. The word "body" is always surrounded in his poems with the same halo as the word "soul" in the works of other poets—which did not prevent him from singing the soul too. He thus continually hesitates between the body and the soul, between the seen and the unseen. His poetry is a constant attempt at combining them and reconciling spirit and matter. "Melange mine own," he called it in "Starting from Paumanok," and he rightly proclaimed: "I am the poet of the Body and I am the poet of the Soul." However, as he grew older, he tended to describe the world in terms of spiritual monism, like the German idealists—in "Passage to India" in particular. But, even in his old-age poems, he kept referring to the equality of matter and spirit.

The reason he felt this duality so vividly was that he was both a sensualist and a mystic. His body apparently vibrated at the least contact with the physical world. His exceptionally acute senses were perpetual sources of wonder and joy. "Seeing, hearing, feeling are miracles," he affirmed. His tactile sensations were especially intense: "I will go to the bank of the wood and become undisguised and naked, / I am mad for it to be in contact with me," he exclaimed at the beginning of "Song of Myself," and he described himself as "the caresser of life." He even listed more obscure sensations as sources of pleasure: his "respiration and inspiration," "the beating of [his] heart, the passing of blood and air through [his] lungs."

Besides these sensations denoting an exceptional hypersensitivity, Whitman was subject to mystical ecstasies. He describes one in "Song of Myself":

> I mind how once we lay such a transparent summer
>   morning,
> How you settled your head athwart my hips and gently
>   turn'd over upon me . . .
> Swiftly arose and spread the peace and knowledge that pass
>   all the arguments of the earth,
> And I know that the hand of God is the promise of my own,

> And that all the men ever born are also my brothers, and
>   the women my sisters and lovers,
> And that a kelson of the creation is love . . .

William James, in *The Varieties of Religious Experience* quotes this passage as a "classical example" of a true mystical state, because of, first, its ineffability, second, its "noetic" quality (it is the revelation of truths which cannot be proved rationally), third, its transiency, and fourth, the passivity it implies, since Whitman feels as if he were grasped and held by a superior power.

Mysticism may eventually lead to the complete dissolution of the self in the (over)soul of the world, but it was not so with Whitman. He regarded life as a two-way process: communion and fusion on the one hand, absorption and distinction on the other. The self now melts away like the tail of a comet by merging with God, now on the contrary absorbs, annexes the world to itself, and thus acquires a distinct "identity." "And these [external things] tend inward to me and I tend outward to them," Whitman tells us. He is "partaker of influx and efflux," "one of that centripetal and centrifugal gang."

Leaves of Grass also implies the dramatic coexistence of two apparently irreconcilable elements: optimism and pessimism. At first sight, it is the expression of an absolute optimism: "How perfect the earth is, and the minutest thing upon it / What is called good is perfect, and what is called sin is just as perfect," he claims in "To Think of Time." He regarded evil merely as an accident, a stage through which things have to pass before they reach perfection, whereas good is a permanent and indestructible part of the central essence of the world. But there were moments when he doubted it and thought that maybe evil would triumph and his soul, his "identity" would be destroyed forever. He sang

> Of the Terrible Doubt of Appearances,
> Of the uncertainty after all, that we may be deluded,
> That may-be reliance and hope are but speculations after all,
> That may-be identity beyond the grave is a beautiful fable
>   only.

Whitman nevertheless did not give way to despair. Though he let some traces of his doubts subsist, *Leaves of Grass* basically expresses his unshakable confidence that the essential meaning of the world "is not chaos or death—it is form, union, plan—it is eternal life—it is Happiness."

Whitman's ambition was not only to sing his self, his doubts, and his hopes, but also "to utter the word Democratic, the word En-Masse." *Leaves of Grass* is the expression of his passionate attachment to the fundamental democratic principles: liberty, equality, fraternity:

> In all people I see myself, none more and not one a barley-
>   corn less . . .
> O such themes—equalities! O divine average! . . .
> All is eligible to all,
> All is for individuals, all is for you.

He extended these rights to women as well as men, proclaiming, for instance: "I am the poet of the woman the same as the man, / And I say it is as great to be a woman as to be a man." His democratic faith, however, was another source of torments and doubts. Reality often disappointed him and made him despair of ever seeing his ideal come true. Yet he never gave up hope. He always thought that democracy was "the destin'd conqueror," and her "spreading mantle "would one day cover the world," as he boldly prophesied in "By Blue Ontario's Shore."

Democracy raised another problem for Whitman. He realized that it might lead to a leveling of all individuals. But he reacted against this in three ways. First, by exalting liberty to the point of anarchy: "Resist much, obey little," he recommended. Second, by insisting that each individual is an end in himself, not a means to an end—that each individual counts, a principle which he developed in *Democratic Vistas* under the name "personalism." Third, by praising great individuals, i.e., leaders like Lincoln who never forgot that they were only the representatives of the people, or great scientists and engineers, or prophets and poets like himself. He thus eventually succeeded in celebrating himself and democracy in the same breath.

His interest in "Modern Man" led him also to celebrate an aspect of modern civilization that few poets had seen fit to mention in verse before him: science and industry—in conformity with Emerson's recommendation. He sang modern inventions with unqualified enthusiasm, whereas other poets, like Sidney Lanier, cursed "the hell-colored smoke of the factories." It was Whitman who, for the first time, undertook to sing both nature and the cities. His *Leaves of Grass* managed to grow even on "the populous pavements" of Manhattan.

For Whitman, the poet is essentially a seer and a prophet. By "Prophet" he meant "one whose mind bubbles up and pours forth as a fountain, from inner, divine spontaneities revealing God. Prediction is a very minor part of prophecy." ("Death of Thomas Carlyle," *Specimen Days*). In other words, like all romantics, he believed in inspiration. Being God's mouthpiece, his aim was not to invent tales of love or war like epic, tragic, or narrative poets (Longfellow in particular). He sang only the glory and wonder of the world. In short, he was exclusively a lyric poet inspired by "the Kosmic Spirit," which made him see "parts as parts but with a feeling of the whole," as Wordsworth said. Whitman used almost the same words: "I will not make poems with reference to parts, / But I will make poems with reference to ensemble." Indeed, as *Leaves of Grass* shows, Whitman never perceived anything without immediately becoming aware of its cosmic content, of the infinity of space and time surrounding it.

He deliberately trained and cultivated this cosmic sense, as the following note found among his papers proves:

> Abstract yourself from this book; realize where you are at present located, the point you stand at that is now to you the centre of all. Look up overhead, think of space stretching out, think of all the unnumbered orbs wheeling safely there invisible to us by day, some visible by night. . . . Spend some minutes faithfully in this exercise. Then again realize yourself upon the earth, at the particular point you now occupy. Which way stretches the north and what countries, seas, etc.? Which way the south? Which way the east? Which way the west? Seize these firmly in your mind, pass freely over im-

mense distances. Turn your face a moment thither. Fix definitely the direction and the idea of the distances of separate sections of your own country, also of England, the Mediterranean Sea, Cape Horn, the North Pole, and such like distant places. . . .

These are true spiritual exercises which Whitman undoubtedly practiced in order to reach a state of grace. He integrated some of them in *Leaves of Grass*. Whenever he draws up long inventories of towns, rivers, and so on—catalogues, as they are usually called—he simply tries to realize himself and make us realize in our turn the immensity of the universe—with the help, at times, of astronomy and geology.

Everything being an inseparable part of the whole in his poetic world, all that exists is a wonderful miracle. If we are to believe him, "The bull and bug [are] never worshipped half enough, / Dung and dirt [are] more admirable than was dreamed." For, he assures us, "the majesty and beauty of the world are latent in any iota of the world." The great merit of his art is precisely to rehabilitate the humblest scenes by surrounding them with a halo of infinity, to make us feel, in particular, the miraculous character of the most banal blades of grass.

In order to achieve this and wake up the reader's dormant sense of wonder, Whitman devised a method of his own and invented a new style—a mixture of the *Baghavat Gita* and the *New York Herald*, as Emerson defined it, an incongruous combination of prosaic banalities and mystical effusions, of lyrical flights and colloquial phrases. When he succeeded in fusing these heterogeneous elements, he metamorphosed reality into something rich and strange, matter was dissolved, trees made "liquid," and all contours fluid. Where discords subsist in his style, they are not due solely to the crudeness of his journalistic training. They result from the duality of his point of view on the world. Sometimes he places himself on the plane of the senses and describes the "seen" in simple and direct terms. Sometimes, as a mystic, he transcends physical appearances and tries to suggest the "unseen." "I help myself to material and immaterial," he said. This explains the coexistence in his poetry of plain descriptive passages and of obscure lines in which he attempted to translate the mysterious "hieroglyphics" which surrounded him. In other words, he endeavored to express the inexpressible, an impossible task. As early as 1855, however, he understood that in order to evoke "transcendent reality" he had to be "indirect and not direct." He therefore tried to suggest the inexpressible by means of images, since "the unseen is proved by the seen," and by means of symbols, since there are mysterious correspondences between the material and the spiritual worlds. In this respect, he was a forerunner of the Symbolists.

What disconcerted Whitman's contemporaries most was less his style than the strange verse medium he had chosen. It was sometimes vaguely reminiscent of the Bible—or Martin Tupper's *Proverbial Philosophy,* but it was nevertheless an entirely new kind of free verse which Whitman meant for the eye rather than for the ear (he said so himself), and in which the music was deliberately sacrificed to the contents. As his manuscripts show, the starting point was always a prose fragment to which he afterward gave a certain lilt. Yet, even the earliest *Leaves of Grass* are not so formless as they may seem at first. The long end-stopped lines conform to a twofold metrical scheme: on the one hand, a system of syntactic parallelisms of reiterations (sometimes called "thought-rhythm") which binds the lines into stanzas, thus replacing the traditional patterns; on the other hand, an ascending or loosely iambic rhythm broken by caesuras at irregular intervals and sometimes reinforced by alliterations.

Later, in *Drump-Taps* and in the poems which followed, music played a more important part. The iambic rhythm became stricter and Whitman sought more and more frequently to obtain effects of imitative harmony, as in "Out of the Cradle Endlessly Rocking" and "When Lilacs Last in the Dooryard Bloom'd." He even revived traditional rhymes by multiplying verbal forms in -ing at the end of lines and half-lines—sometimes at the cost of inversions of which in principle he disapproved.

On the whole, however, Whitman's poetry depends more on "thought-rhythm," that is to say, on the dynamic and restless urge of an inspiration springing from his secret tensions and dichotomies, than on music proper. He realized it himself and, despite the mocking-bird in "Out of the Cradle Endlessly Rocking" and the thrush in "When Lilacs Last in the Dooryard Bloom'd," he rightly claimed:

> I have not so much emulated the birds that musically *sing,*
> I have abandon'd myself to *flights,* broad circles,
> The hawk, the sea-gull have far more possess'd me than the
>   canary or mocking-bird [of Longfellow and Poe],
> I have not felt to warble and trill, however sweetly,
> I have felt to soar in freedom and in the fullness of power,
>   joy, volition.

In the last analysis, whether we consider the matter or the manner, *Leaves of Grass* appears as the work of a poet who deliberately turned his back on conventions and traditions, who boldly dared to go forward along the open roads of the world, and even beyond, through lands which Freud had not yet mapped, into countries where no Surrealist had yet ventured. Like the pioneers whose intrepidity he sang in one of his best-known poems, he was impelled by a restless urge to explore the frontiers of his self and to exploit its latent possibilities in imagination. He thus built at once an immortal book of poetry and what W. B. Yeats called an "artificial personality," full of contradictions and perplexities which he never attempted completely to eliminate or conceal. He passionately searched for God as well as for his inner self and roamed through the infinity of space and time, now full of exuberance and exaltation when he thought he had found ground for faith, now depressed and afraid when it seemed to him that his destination was chaos and nothingness. His poems express with perfect candor his wavering between hope and despair, his hesitations between matter and spirit, optimism and pessimism, the love of life and the attraction of death, liberty and authority, the individual and the masses. The vitality of his poetry comes from this dramatic clash of dialectical opposites. Theses and antitheses constantly conflict with each other. *Leaves of Grass* is a dynamic or, as Whitman would have said, an agonistic attempt at a synthesis. It throbs and palpitates. Who touches it does indeed touch a man.

Notes

1. This is a faithful echo of Emerson's own statement: "Suppose you should contradict yourself; what then?" *Essays, First Series* (London: Routledge, 1893), p. 58.

3.

The Quiddity and Liquidity
of *Leaves of Grass*

Images, however beautiful [. . .] do not themselves characterize the
poet. They become proofs of original genius only as far as they are
modified by a predominant passion; or by associated thoughts or
images awakened by that passion.

—Coleridge

A poet's imagination has a life of its own which escapes him. Like a
plant it lives both above ground and underground. Above ground
it feeds on *air* and tries to capture the energy of the sun's *fire*.
Underground, its roots suck *water* and grope for minerals in the
bosom of the *earth*. Our bodies—and especially a poet's body—constantly dream of the four basic elements on which our lives depend. For our unconscious is not haunted exclusively by phalluses,
as psychoanalysts would like us to believe. We also have a vegeta-
ble life, and images of air, fire, water, and earth inevitably constitute the backdrop of our interior universe and keep changing
like a cloudscape. Gaston Bachelard was probably the first system-
atic explorer of this zone of the poetic imagination, which he called
"material imagination," since it deals only with matter, or "dynamic imagination" because of its constant and irrepressible activity among our underthoughts. He was a philosopher by
profession and originally specialized in the study of scientific methods. Medieval alchemy brought him into contact with pre-rational
modes of thought and pre-Socratic systems—with Thales, who believed that water was the primary stuff of which everything is

31

made; Anaximenes, for whom it was air; Heraclitus, who preferred fire; and Empedocles, for whom the world resulted from a combination of these three elements, plus earth. Alchemists thought along the same lines. They did not reason scientifically. They were dreamers and their dreams were of matter and the four elements which they thought they could transmute into each other. They were persuaded they could change any substance, however base, "into something rich and strange." In short, they were poets, but they dealt with materials instead of words. Realizing the essential identity of poetry and alchemy as far as their aims and methods were concerned, Bachelard undertook to study poetry as a form of alchemy and, over the years, wrote a series of books on the rôle played by the four elements in the imagination of poets: *La Psychanalyse du Feu, L'Eau et Les Rêves, L'Air et les Songes, La Terre et les Rêveries de la Volonté, La Terre et les Rêveries du Repos.* Though he never wrote a line of poetry himself, he was a poet as well as a philosopher. And he looked the part. In his old age, he resembled Whitman more and more with his flowing white beard, the geniality with which he chatted with neighbors and shopkeepers in the Latin Quarter, when he emerged from a room as cluttered with books and papers as the Good Gray Poet's in Mickle Street.

Bachelard's approach, though, is not without its dangers, for reading poems merely to inventory and analyze the water, fire, air, and earth imagery which they contain, regardless of their form and other aspects of their contents, amounts to reducing them all to a common denominator. It tends to emphasize resemblances and obliterate differences between poets. To some extent, it even levels them, since no poet can write poetry without making reference to one or more of the four elements. All poets are equal in this respect: they all treat the same fundamental subject. But every one of them has his own formula and mixes his four basic ingredients in his own way. The proportions vary from one to the other, and there are probably as many combinations as there are fingerprints. For no poet believes in just one element. If one did, he would be a Sherwood Anderson grotesque. He would go around shouting: "The world is on fire!" like Joe Welling in *Winesburg, Ohio.* He would not be a poet, but a monomaniac.

The greatest advantage of Bachelard's method, however, is that it enables us to observe the continuity of the imaginative process *in vitro*. Elemental images come and go, but, when they disappear from sight, they do not cease to exist altogether, they follow secret underground passages until their next resurgence, like "Alph, the sacred river," which ran in Xanadu "through caverns measureless to man." (Whitman himself refers to his poems as "subterranean sea-rills making for the sea," in "As Consequent, etc.," 1. 4). Such images have a life of their own. They are not sought by the poet, they are not literary reminiscences. They are not supplied ready made by his fancy or his memory, but spring from the very depths of his being. They are lifelong obsessions, which explains their recurrence or even permanence. Their presence is thus the best guarantee of a poet's genuineness and the gauge of his sincerity.

Walt Whitman, of course, was no exception to the rule. He was quite aware of the existence and importance of the four elements— even though he knew enough science to realize that they were not the ultimate elements of the physical world from a scientific point of view.

> Air, soil, water, fire—those are words,
> I myself am a word with them—my qualities interpenetrate
>   with theirs, my name is nothing to them,
> Though it were told in the three thousand languages, what
>   would air, soil, water, fire, know of my name?

He declared at the beginning of "A Song of the Rolling Earth" (sec 1, 11. 10-12), listing the four elements as if they were the sum total of the universe. But originally, in 1856, the poem began with two lines:

> *Earth,* round rolling, compact—suns, moons, animals—all
>   these are words,
> *Watery,* vegetable, sauroid advances—being, premonitions,
>   lispings of the future—these are vast words.

In the same year, in "By Blue Ontario's Shore" (which was then entitled "O Poem of Many in One"), he similarly limited his list of elements to two: of the ideal Bard of the New World (in other words, himself), he said that he incorporated "substances, *earth, water,* animals, trees . . ." (sec. 6, l. 4).[1] He was thus quite conscious of the very special place that water occupied in his poetry in the form of fresh as well as salt water. His is a restless kind of water, the very opposite of Poe's opaque, heavy, dead, <u>bituminous</u> water. Whitman's fresh water flows freely, generously all over his "Rolling Earth": "many a stately river flowing and many a jocund brook" ("The Return of Heroes," sec. 7, l. 17). He takes us "where the brook puts out of the roots of the old tree and flows to the meadow" ("Song of Myself," sec. 33, l. 26), for Long Island was an "Isle of sweet brooks of drinking-water . . ." ("Paumanok," l. 4). But he also loves and sings the mighty tidal rivers which encircle Manhattan:

> I loved well those cities [Manhattan and Brooklyn], loved
>   well the stately and rapid river [the East River] . . . .
> ("Crossing Brooklyn Ferry," sec. 4, l. 2)

He did indeed love the "hasty current," the power and dynamism of the East River:

> Flow on, river! flow with the flood-tide and ebb with the
>   ebb-tide! (Ibid., sec. 9, l. 1)

Its "gladness" refreshed him:

> Just as you are refreshed by the gladness of the river and the
>   bright flow, I was refreshed. (Ibid., sec. 3, l. 5).

He imagined himself "laughing and skipping and running" "with the spring waters" of the great Southwestern rivers ("Our Old Feuillage," l. 70), "singing with brooks," or changed into lashing rain like Shelley's cloud:

> . . . I am that which unseen comes and sings, sings, sings,
> Which bubbles in brooks and scoots in showers on the land.
>   ("Song of the Banner at Daybreak," ll. 42-43)

When he stops occasionally for a brief rest, it is to glimpse upon the Great Lakes, "the huge oval lakes" hanging from the belt which ties "the compact lands" of the United States "at the hips" ("Our Old Feuillage," l. 10), "Huron's belt of mighty lakes" ("Election Day, November 1888," l. 4). He had seen the Great Lakes in 1848 on his way back from New Orleans (and Niagara Falls) and had no doubt been duly impressed, but he had seen them as a tourist, he had not lived near them or with them. They were a series of images in his memory, which he could leaf through, as it were, but they were not a part of himself, he had not absorbed them, and that is why they are mentioned only in passing and described as they appear on a map. They were materials which his fancy could play with, but his imagination ignored them. On the contrary, the small nameless ponds on the banks of which he had played or mused as a child on Long Island made him wonder at the extraordinary transparency of the water and the strange creatures which lived curiously suspended in it as in the air, so close at hand and yet out of reach, in an entirely different world:

> And the fish suspending themselves so curiously below there,
>   and the beautiful curious liquid,
> And the water-plants with their curious flat heads, all
>   became part of him. ("There Was a Child Went Forth,"
>   ll. 9-10)

Unlike Thoreau, who was a landlubber, to whom Walden Pond served the purpose of a sea, and unlike William Carlos Williams, who responded only to the Passaic River, Whitman, who lived within sight and earshot of the ocean during all his childhood and youth, dreamed of the sea and sea water even more often than of brooks and ponds. He pointed out himself in *Specimen Days* that Long Island, "Paumanok," as he preferred to call it "to give the spot its original name," was "worth fully and particularly investigating, stretching east [. . .] 120 miles altogether—on the north Long Island Sound, a beautiful, varied and picturesque series of inlets, 'necks' and sea-like expansions, for a hundred miles to Orient Point. On the ocean side, the great south bay dotted with countless hummocks [. . .] now and then, as at Rockaway and far east along the Hamptons, the beach makes right on the island, the sea dashing up without intervention [. . .] a long history of wrecks tragedies, some even of late years. As a youngster, I was in the atmosphere and tradition of many of these wrecks—of one or two almost an observer. Off Hempstead beach, for example, was the loss of the ship 'Mexico' in 1840 [alluded to in "The Sleepers" in *Leaves of Grass*]." [2] And he added, insisting on the importance of all these early experiences: "As I write, the whole experience comes back to me after the lapse of forty and more years—the soothing rustle of the waves, and the saline smell—boyhood's times, the clam-digging, barefoot, and with trowsers roll'd up—hauling down the creek—the perfume of the sedge-meadows—the hay-boat, and the chowder and fishing excursions; or, of later years, little voyages down and out of New York bay, in the pilot boats. Those same later years, also, while living in Brooklyn (1836-50) I went regularly every week in the mild seasons down to Coney Island, at that time a long, bare unfrequented shore, which I had all to myself, and where I loved, after bathing, to race up and down the hard sand, and declaim Homer or Shakespere to the surf and seagulls by the hour." [3]

He thus absorbed the sea through all his senses: sight, hearing, smell, and touch, during at least the first thirty years of his life. It haunted him ever after. Even as a boy, when he was the barefoot "outsetting bard" he described in "Out of the Cradle Endlessly Rocking," he had, he said, "the fancy, the wish, to write a piece, perhaps a poem, about the sea-shore—that suggesting, dividing line, contact, junction, the solid marrying the liquid—that curious, lurking something (as doubtless every objective form finally becomes to the subjective spirit,) which means far more than its mere sight, grand as that is—blending the real and the ideal, and each made portion of the other." [4]

Even in those early days, he was, by instinct as it were, a transcendentalist to whom material surfaces were only appearances and the terminus of some mysterious, intangible, but absolutely real spiritual presence. He felt connected with it by mysterious ties: "What is it in us, arous'd by those indirections and directions?" he wondered. "That spread of waves and gray-white beach, salt, monotonous, senseless [. . .] so indescribably comforting, even this winter day—grim, yet so delicate-looking, so spiritual—striking emotional depths, subtler than all the poems, paintings, music, I have ever read, seen, heard." [5]

This central presence, this mysterious embodiment, or even incarnation, of God in the sea is *the* central motif of *Leaves of Grass,* if we are to believe this passage in *Specimen Days:*

> *Once [at Montauk Point] (by the old light-house, nothing but sea-tossings in every direction as far as the eye could reach,) I remember well, I felt that I must one day write a book expressing this liquid, mystic theme. Afterward, I recollect, how it came to me that instead of any special lyrical or epical or literary attempt, the sea-shore should be an invisible* influence, *a pervading gauge and tally for me, in my composition!* [6]

So, though it is not always in the foreground this marriage of water and earth, and, above all, "this mystic, liquid theme" is the true subject of *Leaves of Grass,* which, as he pointed out in one of the "Inscriptions," "In Cabin'd Ships at Sea," is "ocean's poem" (l. 16), "not a reminiscence of the land alone" (l. 18). "See on the one side the Western Sea, and on the other the Eastern Sea, how they advance and retreat upon my poems as upon their own shores" ("Starting from Paumanok," sec. 18, l. 4), he noted in 1860, when the theme became particularly prominent and fully explicit, since it was in the third edition of *Leaves of Grass,* published in that year, that we find such poems as "Out of the Cradle Endlessly Rocking," "As I Ebb'd with the Ocean of Life," "The World Below the Brine," and "Facing West from California's Shores."

Sea water was first for him that water in which he loved to wade as a child on the shores of Paumanok. Wading "with naked feet along the beach just in the edge of the water," was one of the miracles of which he drew up a list in the 1856 *Leaves of Grass.*

"To me the sea is a continual miracle," he added, "The fishes that swim—the rocks—the motion of the waves—the ships with men in them" (Miracles," ll. 5, 21-22).

In order to be in more intimate contact with it, he often swam in it. He was no athletic swimmer, however, like the "beautiful gigan-

tic swimmer swimming naked through the eddies of the sea" whose
death he has described in "The Sleepers" (sec. 3). His style was
closer to that of Coleridge than to that of Swinburne. Though, in
"Song of Myself," he exhorted his reader to strike out for the open
sea—

> Long have you timidly waded holding a plank by the shore,
> Now I will you to be a bold swimmer,
> To jump off in the midst of the sea, rise again, nod to me,
>   shout, and laughingly dash with your hair (sec. 46, II.
>   31-33),

in practice, he preferred to hug the shore and float lazily rather
than swim. Being "the caresser of life" [7] with "instant conductors"
all over his body,[8] he surrendered to the caresses of the water with
total passivity and was rewarded by voluptuous sensations:

> You sea: I resign myself to you also—I guess what you mean,
> I behold from the beach your crooked inviting fingers,
> I believe you refuse to go back without feeling of me,
> We must have a turn together, I undress, hurry me out of
>   sight of the land,
> Cushion me soft, rock me in billowy drowse,
> Dash me with amorous wet, I can repay you.[9]

The sea bathed him in bliss, to take up his own expression in
"Proud Music of the Storm" (sec. 4, 1. 6). He equated making love
with swimming in the sea: "I do not ask any more delight, I swim
as in a sea," he claimed in "I Sing the Body Electric" (sec. 4, 1. 5).
In a way, he and the sea were lovers—of unspecified and varying
sexes, the sea, like himself, being now female, now male, as when,
in "Spontaneous Me," he describes

> The souse upon me of my lover the sea, as I lie willing and
>   naked. (I. 35)

The sea is love, the sea is life to him, it flows and runs and rushes
perpetually. Besides, since the same salt water with which it souses
the bathers runs through our veins and carries the male's semen,

those "limitless limpid jets of love hot and enormous, quivering jelly of love," [10] "the sobbing liquid of life" ("Song of Myself," sec. 42, 1. 15), he feels physically "integral with the sea, as he says, because it is "the brine of life." [11] He is thus led to attribute to the sea the powers which most primitive people assigned to an Earth Goddess (Demeter). Whereas he calls the land "my father"—a rather unflattering identification, when one knows how Whitman usually rated his father, he again and again treats the sea as a universal mother. She is "the old mother," swaying to and fro, singing her husky song "on the beach at night alone," [12] "the fierce old mother incessantly moaning," "the savage old mother" [13]—a rather sinister and ominous figure and quite different from his own mother, contrary to what we might have expected, but Whitman's Sea Goddess is a kind of *Janus Bifrons:* one of her faces expresses love and kindness, while the other frowns and threatens. The reason for this ambivalent attitude is that the sea is both life and death. It is both a loving life-giver and a cruel destroyer, a "dark mother always gliding near with soft feet." [14] Whitman's thoughts about the sea implicitly follow a curious Hegelian dialectic. Thesis: the sea is life; antithesis: the sea is death; synthesis: death is not to be feared; it is not the cold and implacable male God of tradition, but "a lovely and soothing" Goddess, a "strong deliveress." There can be nothing but praise "for the sure-enwinding arms of cool-enfolding death," and one can "joyously sing the dead,

Lost in the loving floating ocean of thee,

Laved in the flood of thy bliss, O death." [15]

This was not, properly speaking, the conclusion of logical reasoning, but rather the outcome of a slowly evolving meditation or reverie on the sea, based on sensations and impressions rather than on concepts, founded on materials, not on ideas. This position was eventually reached by the poet after the Civil War, when he found confirmation of what he claimed in 1860 that he had heard the sea tell him one night as a boy "on Paumanok's gray beach," when,

Delaying not, hurrying not,

it had whispered to him, lisped to him "the low and delicious word death," "the word of the sweetest song and all songs." [16] On that occasion, it was "hissing melodious," Whitman said—an oxymoron which already marked the beginning of a reconciling synthesis.

All was not bliss, however, in Whitman's life. He could not always merge voluptuously in the watery element. There were "hours continuing, long, sore, and heavy-hearted," [17] "sullen and suffering hours," "hours of [. . .] torment" when in particular he was tortured by sexual desire, "the hungry gnaw" which ate him "night and day" and which, for all kinds of reasons, he could not satisfy as he wanted. He could not liberate the "pent-up aching rivers" of his sexuality, though, with "voice resonant," he boldly sang "the phallus," "the song of procreation." [18] There were thus times when it seemed to him that life was meaningless and he was drifting without destination in a chaotic world.[19] For all his transcendentalist fervor, he knew that practically the world is far from perfect. The existence of evil did not escape him and he did not seek to deny. it. He sometimes even probed in imagination all the turpitudes of the world. It was then that he declared:

> Agonies are one of my changes of garments.[20]
> The pleasures of heaven are with me and the pains of hell
>   are with me.[21]

He was as much aware as any pessimistic thinker of the existence of evil both in himself and in the external world, and came close to calling his poems *Flowers of Evil* like Baudelaire. He hesitated for a time between "flames of evil" and "drops of evil," between fire and water, and finally adopted neither of the two, though, by choosing *Leaves of Grass* for a title he ultimately inclined toward water.

Water helped him to express the tragic sadness as well as the wonder of the world. The sea, it often seemed to him, was as restless and as much tormented by unsatisfied desires as himself:

> O madly the sea pushes upon the land
> With love, with love.[22]
> The wild unrest, the snowy, curling caps—that inbound urge
>   and urge of waves,

Seeking the shores forever.[23]
The limpid liquid within the young man,
The vex'd corrosion, so pensive and so painful,
The torment, the irritable tide that will not be at rest,
The like of the same I feel.[24]

He thought, or dreamed he heard

Ripples of unseen rivers, tides of a current flowing, forever
    flowing,
(Or is it the plashing of tears? the measureless waters of
    human tears?) [25]

He elaborated this theme in his old age in "With Husky-Haughty Lips, O Sea," which concludes with:

Some vast heart, like a planet's, chain'd and chafing in those
    breakers,
By lengthen'd swell, and spasm and panting breath,
And rhythmic rasping of thy sands and waves,

[. . .]
(Sounding, appealing to the sky's deaf ear—but now, rapport
    for once,
A phantom in the night, thy confidant for once,)
The first and last confession of the globe,
Outsurging, muttering from thy soul's abysms,
The tale of cosmic elemental passion,
Thou tellest to a kindred soul.

He had expressed his kinship with a rainstorm at night on the seashore much more mysteriously, though with some pathetic fallacy, in 1867:

On the white shore, dripping, dripping, suck'd in by the
    sand,
Tears, not a star shining, all dark and desolate,
Moist tears from the eyes of a muffled head;

O who is that ghost? that form in the dark with tears?
What shapeless lump is that, bent, crouch'd there on the
    sand?
Streaming tears, sobbing tears, throes, choked with wild
    cries;
O storm, embodied, rising, careering with swift steps along
    the beach!
O wild and dismal nightstorm, with wind—O belching and
    desperate!
O shade so sedate and decorous by day, with calm
    countenance and regulated face,
But away at night, as you fly, none looking—O then the
    unloosen'd ocean,
Of tears! tears! tears![26]

The desperate ghost of this poem is probably no other than the phantom of "Whispers of Heavenly Death," that is to say, the poet himself melting into tears and dissolving in the water of the bliss and the torment of the world.

As he grew older, Whitman became more and more eager to escape from this earth to a world where he would be free of the shackles of matter:

The untold want by life and land ne'er granted,
Now voyager sail thou forth to seek and find,[27]

was the recommendation he addressed to himself in 1871, whereas in all his former poems he was satisfied with traveling inland and, except for a few fishing expeditions, never thought of leaving the safety of the shore when he waded on the beaches of Paumanok. But at the time when he wrote "Passage to India," he dreamed of turning his back on the land and its impurities and sailing (metaphorically) to distant, almost ethereal and immaterial seas where he would be laved and become pure spirit and merge—or rather *bathe*—in God:

O soul thou pleasest me, I thee,
Sailing these seas or on the hills, or waking in the night

Thoughts, silent thoughts, of Time and Space and Death,
    like waters flowing,
Bear me indeed as through the regions infinite,
Whose air I breathe, whose ripples hear, lave all over,
Bathe me O God in thee . . .
Passage, immediate passage! the blood burns in my veins!
Away O soul! hoist instantly the anchor![28]

A psychoanalyst would probably see here mere regressive imagery unconsciously expressing the desire of the poet to take refuge in his mother's womb and return to its pocket of amniotic fluid in order once more to enjoy there the perfect peace and happiness of the *torpid embryo*.[29] The last two words are Whitman's. He used them in a different context in "Song of Myself" when describing his own cosmic genesis:

My *embryo* has never been torpid, nothing could overlay it.
    (sec. 44, 1. 30)

This denial also applies to his conscious life, for this evolution shows that he never looked backward, but forward. He was not craving for a return to a purely material condition, but, on the contrary, was aspiring to the liberation of his soul and its union with the soul of the world. Of course, at this point, a psychoanalyst would again object that this is exactly what is meant by the phrase "regressive process." Everything here depends on whether the reader is a materialist who regards man as an organism governed by tropisms and led by animal instincts, or a spiritualist who, like Teilhard de Chardin, is impatient to reach point Omega at the apex of the noosphere. Though Whitman now wavered between the two positions and now tried to reconcile them, he leaned more and more toward the latter after the Civil War.

As a result of this gradual shift, water, originally one of the four material elements, tends to become in *Leaves of Grass* an immaterial substance, a spirit, God. *Leaves of Grass* celebrates, among other things, the apotheosis of water. Matter is dematerialized and becomes an intangible and indescribable thing. The world is liquefied, so to speak. Everything flows toward the mystic ocean:

All, all toward the mystic ocean tending.[30]

God is liquid. Life is an irresistible current which circulates through all things. And here Whitman's spiritualism joins hands with some of his early intuitions, dating back to his materialistic period, for, as early as 1855, he used in the poem which was to become "Song of Myself" an extraordinary water image, when addressing the earth as "Earth of the slumbering *liquid* trees" (sec. 21, 1. 18). In those early days, it was not God, but matter that was liquid. Trees were fountains. He could have entitled his book "Liquid Leaves of Grass," for water practically had the titular role, even then. He assigned an aquatic origin to all things, which, according to him, had cohered from a nebulous "float," as he called it, that is to say, a sort of vapor or quintessential water floating in space:

> Do you think matter has cohered together from its diffuse
>   float, and the soil is on the surface, and water runs and
>   vegetation sprouts,
> For you only, and not him and her?

he boldly asserted in "I Sing the Body Electric" (sec. 6, ll. 19-20).

> I too had been struck from the float ever held in solution,"

he maintained in "Crossing Brooklyn Ferry" (sec. 5, 1. 9).

> I too have bubbled up, floated the measureless float and
>   been washed on your shores [Paumanok],

he repeated in "As I Ebb'd with the Ocean of Life" (sec. 3, 1. 8).

The world to him was "an eternal float of solution" suspended "here and everywhere," [31] "the float of the sight of things," which flowed into him through his eyes.[32]

From the float which potentially contained him in solution to the mystic ocean toward which he aspired to sail in his old age, Whitman thus spent all his life among "liquid" or "fluid" things, flying "those flights of a *fluid* and swallowing soul," [33] "fluid as

Nature." [34] ("L'âme soluble dans l'âme," [35] said Paul Claudel, in whose poetry water also flows abundantly.) In such a context, all the other elements tend to be underestimated.

Though fire—the fire of energy [36] and, above all, sex—is not completely extinguished in *Leaves of Grass* (for "the sight of the flames maddens [him] with pleasure" [37] when he has a chance to follow a fire engine and watch a fire), as a rule, it does not generate much heat.

> Little you know the subtle electric fire that for your sake is
>   playing within me,

he said (in a poem) to one of the young men he loved,[38] but it was apparently too subtle to be felt. Besides, electricity, in Whitman's poetry, partakes both of fire and water, since it generally takes the form of a current which flows like water. The same is true of the moon, which in *Leaves of Grass* is more full of water than of fire or light. Far from attracting the sea, as it should, it is attracted by it, "the yellow half-moon enlarged, *sagging down*, drooping, the face of the sea almost touching, like a drop of water about to fall." [39] Though Whitman claims he sees "the vast alembic ever working" and knows "the flames that heat the world," [40] even when he has to express passion, he prefers water imagery, as we can observe in "Not Heat Flames Up and Consumes," where the sea waves and the tide soon take the relay of the flames.

This applied to air, too. Water in *Leaves of Grass,* like Nature, abhors a vacuum and immediately fills up any space occupied merely by air. When the poet declares he flies "those flights of a fluid and swallowing soul," one might believe he flies through air. Not at all, for the next line informs us that his "course runs below the soundings of plummets." [41] When he faces facts, Whitman, like everyone else, knows that "This is the common air that bathes the globe," [42] but at night, in the dark, the world puts on a different appearance; in the dark, you escape everyday reality; especially if you are dreaming, as Whitman is in "The Sleepers," and then air turns to water, for "the sleepers [in his dream] are very beautiful as they lie unclothed, / They *flow* hand in hand over the whole earth . . ." (sec. 8, ll. 1-2) curiously suspended in "the beautiful curious liquid,"[1] like the fish he used to observe in the pond as a child. "The Sleepers" is nearly a surrealistic poem. It could almost bear the same title as André Breton's "Le Poisson Soluble," "The Soluble Fish."

The only element which resists dissolution or displacement in Whitman's poetry is earth, the land, which we have already found several times associated with water and on a par with it. Strangely enough, he chose the land to represent his father, whereas in most mythologies and with most poets the father is identified with the sun. But Whitman preferred the land because in his *Weltanschauung* the land was the sea's antagonist along the seashores of the world, and he instinctively associated his mother with the sea. He needed the land, though, insofar as he needed a partner for the sea, but he was not interested in it *per se*. Yet, he had a further use for it, for, in alliance with water it produced the vegetation. Leaves of grass ("blades" would have been too aggressively of the earth earthy) result from the synthesis of earth and water. They contain "blood," he says in "This Compost" (1. 8). Earth and water, also, more simply, produce mud, that "unctuous," health-giving substance in which he bathed in the solitude of Timber Creek after his stroke. In "The Voice of the Rain" he even went so far as to write: "I am the Poem of the Earth, said the Voice of the Rain," thus substituting water for earth.

So water triumphed on all fronts, because it was both material and fluid. It enabled him to keep his promise to write "the most spiritual poems" by making "the poems of materials." [43] He was attracted to it as a child and it became the background of his thoughts and the substance of his dreams. He lived in air, but dreamed in water, if I may say so. In other words, water was the medium of his internal life and became a source of vital images. These images, for all their grounding in reality, are not at all to be taken literally, however. They are metaphors, but metaphors with a core of experience. We can still hear the ripple of Long Island Sound in them, or the howling storms which sometimes beat on the shores of Paumanok, for by a natural association water to him *was* poetry and poetry water. He was sensitive to the melody as well as to the rhythm of the sea:

We feel the long pulsation, ebb and flow of endless motion,

The tones of unseen mystery, the vague and vast suggestion
of the briny world, the liquid-flowing syllables . . .
. . . the melancholy rhythm. . . .[44]

In these lines he was describing both the sea and his own poetry,
which in a way breathes like the sea.

So he was a new Narcissus in the most literal sense. He not only
sang his "Song of Myself" "over the roofs of the world," and loved
being photographed (he probably was the most photographed author of his time) and having his likeness painted and his statue
carved, but he could not detach himself from the water, which sent
him back his reflection (physical and moral). During all his career
as a poet, he was virtually standing on the deck of Brooklyn Ferry,

Look[ing] at the fine centrifugal spokes of light round the
shape of [his] head in the sunlit water. . . .[45]

But he was no static Narcissus like the Narcissus of Greek mythol-
ogy, he was a cosmic and dynamic one,

The current rushing so swiftly and swimming with him far
away,[46]

through the infinity of space and time, from his native Paumanok
to "the mystic ocean" of his dreams, where he was eventually to
disappear forever.

Though we live in air, we are still fundamentally aquatic creatures. We carry our own sea water with us wherever we go inside
our skin in our blood vessels, and, though few of us drink mere
water, water plays a vital part in our lives. In summer, the city
dwellers we have become migrate massively to the seashore and
disport themselves in water, turning more or less successfully into
amphibians, returning to the sea where their remote fishy ancestors
came from, trying to recapture the perfect bliss which, if we are to
believe psychoanalysts, they once enjoyed as embryos in their

mothers' amniotic fluid. We have all somehow retained the nostalgic memory of our original water. The Garden of Eden was actually planted with seaweeds, as Whitman fully realized:

> The world below the brine.
> Forests at the bottom of the sea, the branches and leaves . . .
> Dumb swimmers there among the rocks . . .
> The change thence to the sight here, and to the subtle air
>   breathed by beings like us who walked this sphere. . . .[47]

Though we move externally in air, we all live internally in water and the more sensitive of us, those of us who still trail after them clouds of glory, dimly remember their watery origin, and, like Whitman, constantly dream of it. And that is one of the reasons we respond so well to his *Leaves of Grass* and it wakes such deep echoes in us. To take up André Breton's image, the poet and his reader are "vases communicants," and they communicate invisibly through Jung's *id*—or Yeats's "great memory"—which are no doubt mostly made up of water.

Notes

1. In "Song of Myself," sec. 31, 11. 8-9, he had already developed the same idea: "I find I incorporate gneiss, coal, long-threaded moss, fruits, grain, esculent roots / And am stucco'd with quadrupeds and birds all over."
2. "Paumanok, and my life on it as child and young man," Specimen Days, *The Complete Poetry and Prose of Walt Whitman,* ed. with an introduction by Malcolm Cowley (New York: Pellegrini & Cudahy, 1948), vol. II, p. 8.
3. Ibid., p. 10.
4. "Sea-Shore Fancies," ibid., p. 91.
5. "A Winter Day on the Sea-Beach," ibid., p. 91.
6. "Sea-Shore Fancies," ibid., pp. 91-2.
7. "Song of Myself," sec. 13, l. 8.
8. "Song of Myself," sec. 27, l. 28.
9. "Song of Myself," sec. 22, ll. 1-6.
10. "I Sing the Body Electric," sec. 5, l. 9.
11. "Song of Myself," sec. 22, ll. 9, 11.
12. "On the Beach at Night Alone," ll. 1-2.
13. "Out of the Cradle Endlessly Rocking," ll. 131-41.
14. "When Lilacs Last in the Dooryard Bloom'd," sec. 14, l. 36.
15. Ibid., ll. 28-43.

16. "Out of the Cradle Endlessly Rocking," ll. 165-83.
17. See the poem beginning with these words.
18. "From Pent-Up Aching Rivers," ll. 1, 4, 11.
19. Cf. the variant reading of "Out of the Cradle Endlessly Rocking" (ll. 158 and following) in Emory Holloway's Inclusive Edition of *Leaves of Grass,* p. 638.
20. "Song of Myself," sec. 33, l. 136.
21. Ibid., sec. 21, l. 2.
22. "Out of the Cradle Endlessly Rocking," ll. 77-78.
23. "From Montauk Point," ll. 4-5.
24. "Spontaneous Me," ll. 27-30.
25. "Whispers of Heavenly Death," ll. 4-5.
26. "Tears," l. 3 to the end.
27. "The Untold Want."
28. "Passage to India," sec. 8, ll. 13-18, sec. 9, ll. 19-20.
29. Cf. Stephen A. Black, *Whitman's Journeys Into Chaos—A Psychoanalytic Study of the Poetic Process* (Princeton, N.J.: Princeton University Press, 1975), xv + 255 pp.
30. "As Consequent, etc.," l. 15.
31. "Crossing Brooklyn Ferry," sec., l. 7.
32. "A Song of the Open Road," sec., l. 14.
33. "Song of Myself," sec. 33, l. 91.
34. "So Long!" l. 25.
35. "Cinq Grandes Odes," "cinquième ode: La Maison fermée," in *Oeuvre Poétique* (Paris: Pléiade Ed., 1957), p. 283.
36. See: "For not all matter is fuel to heat, impalpable flame, the essential life of the earth. . . ," "Starting from Paumanok," sec. 8, l. 7.
37. "A Song of Joys," l. 21.
38. "O You Whom I Often and Silently Come," l. 3.
39. "Out of the Cradle Endlessly Rocking," l. 135.
40. "The Mystic Trumpeter," sec. 5, l. 7.
41. "Song of Myself," sec. 33, ll. 91-92.
42. Ibid., sec. 17, l. 6.
43. "Starting from Paumanok," sec. 6, l. 3.
44. "In Cabin'd Ships, at Sea," ll. 12-14. Cf. also, "Song at Sunset," l. 35: "How the water sports and sings! (surely it is alive!)"
45. "Crossing Brooklyn Ferry," sec. 3, l. 14.
46. "Crossing Brooklyn Ferry," sec. 2, l. 5.
47. "The World Below the Brine," ll. 1, 2, 5, 10.

4.

Whitman's Transcendental Humor

Is there such a thing as Walt Whitman's humor? Opinions differ. Constance Rourke annexed him and included his name in her inventory of *American Humor* for two reasons, it seems: because he followed Emerson's advice and hitched his wagon to a star, and because he heard America singing. These, however, are not very convincing arguments, and it is not surprising that Jesse Bier, on the contrary, in his *Rise and Fall of American Humor,* should make a case for Whitman's total humorlessness.[1] And yet, it was Richard Chase's contention that " 'Song of Myself' is on the whole comic in tone and that although the poem's comic effects are of universal significance, they often take the specific form of American humor." [2] Whom are we to believe?

A priori, there seems to be an absolute incompatibility between humor and lyric poetry, and more than an s's difference between "comic" and "cosmic." When I first opened Chase's book and happened on the word "comic" where I expected "cosmic," I couldn't believe my eyes and thought it was a printer's error, until I found the baffling word a second and a third and an nth time, for, whereas humor consists in playing with ludicrous contrasts, lyric poetry sings the emotions of the self facing the universe (and/or nothingness), and at first sight, they seem to have little in common. Yet, great lyric—or dramatic—poets have succeeded in combining them. Shakespeare, Jean-Paul Richter, Dylan Thomas, and Paul Claudel are, each in his own way, perfect illustrations of this possibility. Claudel even went so far as to say: "La farce est la forme exaspérée du lyrisme et l'expression héroïque de la joie de vivre. . . ." [3] He was right. The same exuberance and exhilaration is at the root of both forms of expression. The poet and the humorist react with the same passion and intensity to the beauty and horror of life. So the same writer may, either in turn or simultaneously, sing and laugh, rhapsodize or mock.

Whitman, for his part, was not a pure poet. True, he stripped lyric poetry of all its traditional trappings in *Leaves of Grass,* but he discovered lyricism quite late in life. He started as a prose writer of the lowest order (i.e., as a journalist) and he never ceased to write prose—and that is where he relegated the impurities which would otherwise have encumbered and corrupted his poetry. His early prose, as everyone knows, is a rather insipid mixture of maudlin sentimentality and sententious moralizing in the worst tradition of eighteenth-century English essayists. But he also occasionally tried to write in the vein of eighteenth-century English humorists, using that combination of "wit and love" which, according to Thackeray, was the essence of English humor—at least in that period.[4] For the entertainment of his "gentle reader," [5] he thus amiably descanted on young smokers in the columns of the *Long Island Democrat:*

> There is something very majestic, truly, in seeing a human being with a long roll of black leaves held between his teeth, and projecting eight or ten inches before him. It has been said by some satirical individual that a fishing-rod is a thing with a hook at one extremity, and a fool at the other: it may with much more truth be affirmed, that a segar, generally, has a *smoky fire* at one end, and a *conceited spark* at the other.[6]

There was more love and less irony in his considerations on loaferism since he was no smoker himself, but an inveterate loafer:

> How I do love a loafer! Of all human beings, none equals
> your genuine, inbred, unvarying loafer. Now when I say
> loafer, I *mean* loafer; not a fellow who is lazy by fits and
> starts—who today will work his twelve or fourteen hours, and
> to-morrow doze and idle. I stand up for no such half-way
> business. Give me your calm, steady, philosophick son of indo-
> lence; one that doesn't swerve from the beaten track; a man
> who goes the undivided beast. To such an one I doff my
> beaver.[7]

In such sketches he may have been trying to emulate Charles
Lamb, whose essays he loved and praised, referring in the *Brooklyn
Eagle* to "the pleasant Elia, the delicate-humored." [8] He even resorted to Charles Lamb's hallmark, the hyphen, in order to under-
line, as it were, his humorous intention.

He also wrote variations on the theme of "snoring made music":

> You are tired and long for rest. You get into the confines of
> sleep, when one of your fellow lodgers begins to snore: softly at
> first—a little higher—then a little stronger, till finally it resem-
> bles the grumbling of distant thunder. . . . Presently another
> joins in. His snoring is decidedly as disagreeable as the first,
> but his style is totally different—it sounds something like the
> puffings of a steam engine. . . .

On this occasion, Whitman even coined the humorously pedan-
tic or pedantically humorous noun: "snorification," [9] worthy of his
fellow humorists of the Southwest.

In those days he would sometimes play jokes on his readers, as
when, having no idea for a leader, he expatiated on the weather
with a deadpan face, so to speak, in the columns of the *New York
Aurora,* and triumphantly concluded his disquisitions with:

> Undoubtedly, no person can now have any reason for
> doubting that the weather is, by custom, a legitimate theme
> for persons to exercise their voices (and pens) upon.
>
> The thing is done—the leader is prepared! *Laus Deo!* [10]

No wonder he praised and recommended to his readers a few years later a humorous contemporary of the *Brooklyn Eagle,* "the *John Donkey,* a new quarto illustrated journal of humor and drive-away-careism." "It is rich exceedingly! he added, the number sent us has more broad wit—the real coarse, but deep, true stuff, like Shakespere's (without any indelicacy, however,) own natural comic humor—than any eight pages published, that we have seen." [11]

It is hard to recognize the poet of *Leaves of Grass* when he thus dons the humorist's motley, but this was only a youthful phase. As Horace Traubel very aptly put it: "he played the usual juvenile part in literary mimicry." [12]

He indulged in this harmless pastime especially during a stay in New Orleans, when he wrote for the *Crescent* a series of sketches supposedly composed by Peter Funk, Esq. in which he poked gentle fun at a number of local characters: Timothy Goujon, seller of "a certain species of fish ycleped oysters, vending *viva voce* the inanimate quadrupeds which lay piled up with so much *sang froid* in his boat beside him"; Patrick McDray, the "stout, hardy-looking" teamster from "the swate Isle" across the Ocean; and, above all, Daggerdraw Bowieknife, Esq., "this fearful son of Mars" whose "shooting irons made daylight shine through . . . no less than six hale, hearty men," "always loaded down to the guards with fashionable killing tools." [13]

Like a true humorist, he obviously restrained his indignation when he caricatured that cruel and unscrupulous Southern killer, and preferred to mock rather than vituperate. His Dutch phlegm no doubt helped him to control or hide his feelings. He was not merely imitating contemporary humorists or following a fashion— there *was* a streak of humor in his character, which he retained to the end of his life, though he never showed it again in his prose writings (*Specimen Days* is unrelievedly serious, from beginning to end). It still sometimes cropped up, however, in his conversations with Traubel, his humorless Boswell, who was blissfully unaware of it. Another friend of his old age, Thomas B. Harned, though terribly humorless too, noted: "He had a sense of humor of a quiet kind." [14]

It was of a rather quiet kind indeed, for, at least toward the end of his life he seems to have been quite indifferent to humorists. When Traubel asked him if he had seen Bill Nye and James Whitcomb Riley when they lectured in Philadelphia, he answered:

> As a general thing, I don't enjoy dialect literature: it's rather troublesome to handle: yet Jim took a powerful hold on me: but though I don't care much for the dialect writers myself I acknowledge their validity, value, pertinence: that some of them are remarkably gifted: they indicate, stand for, exemplify, an important phase in our literary development.[15]

On another occasion he was even less sympathetic. To a visitor who asked him what he knew about Bill Nye he answered:

> Nothing—I have never met him. I have very little liking for deliberate wits—for men who start out, with malice prepense to be funny—just as I should distrust deliberate pathos.[16]

In short, he disapproved of humor for humor's sake—of humor as sheer fun—and that is probably why he never took to Mark Twain. Like most of his contemporaries, he regarded him as a mere clown: "I think he mainly misses fire," he said. "He might have been something, he comes near to being something: but he never arrives." [17] On the contrary, Whitman loved and revered Dickens and Carlyle, who were not mere entertainers, but used humor as a means to an end, that end being the indirect (a very Whitmanian term) expression of their reactions to men and things and even of their *Weltanschauung.* In their works, humor is the figure in the carpet, not the whole carpet. Whitman reviewed several of Dickens's books and always praised them. He never mentioned his humor, but concluded one of his reviews with this tribute: "I cannot lose the opportunity of saying how much I love and esteem him for what he has taught me through his writings—and for *the genial influence* [italics mine] that these writings spread around them wherever they go." [18] As for Carlyle, he praised the "strange wild way" of *Sartor Resartus* and its "fiery breath and profundity of meaning—when you delve them out" and the "rapt, weird (grotesque?), style" of *Heroes and Hero-Worship*—though he confessed:

"we would have preferred to get the thoughts of this truly good thinker, in a plainer and more customary garb. No great writer achieves any thing worthy of him, by inventing merely a new style." [19]

Yet, this is precisely what he did himself when he suddenly metamorphosed from a mediocre journalist into a great poet in the 1850s. He did not hesitate to be quaint, "weird (grotesque?)." Humor—though he never used the word—was, after all, part and parcel of his design, one of the figures in the carpet of *Leaves of Grass.* For one thing, he was undeniably a humorist in the eighteenth-century sense: he boldly flung his eccentricity in the face of the world. Who before him ever thought of writing about grass (instead of flowers) and calling it poetry? It was much the same kind of undertaking as writing about the weather in the *New York Aurora* and calling it a leader. What a strange idea too, to call the finished product *Leaves of Grass* and to print it without the author's name or a pseudonym on the title page! and to hide his name in the middle of a poem! and to write in a medium which was neither prose nor verse! and to give no titles to the separate (?) poems! This was clearly a hoax, a mystification rather than a serious book of poetry—the work of a madman, in short, as some of the reviewers concluded in 1855. They were right in a way. They were more alive than we are, anyway, to the scandalous novelty of the book— and to its humorous character.

Humor is a very elusive quality, which defies definition. It consists mostly in discovering, expressing, or appreciating ludicrous or absurdly incongruous elements in ideas or situations. Now is there a more incongruous situation than that of a supposedly omniscient adult being stumped by the very simple question of a child about one of the most common things in the world, grass? Yet it is on this incongruous contrast that *Leaves of Grass* is built, since the major part of the book is an attempt at answering (indirectly) the child's question: "What is the grass?"

This awkward situation, besides, implies the true humorist's sense of the relativity of all values: what is important? what is not? No one can tell. Grass soon appears as a much more important thing than is generally thought. Established religions, on the contrary, are shown to be much less important than their members believed;

> Magnifying and applying come I,
> Outbidding at the start the old cautious hucksters [a rather
>   irreverent way of referring to prophets and founders of
>   religions!]
> Taking myself the exact dimension of Jehovah . . .
> In my portfolio placing Manito loose, Allah on a leaf, the
>   crucifix engraved,
> With Odin and the hideous-faced Mexitli and every idol and
>   image,
> Taking them all for what they are and not a cent more . . .
> (They bore mites as for unfledg'd birds who have now to rise
>   and fly and sing for themselves,) . . . .[20]

Time and space are also mere illusions in his eyes:

> Space and Time! now I see it is true, what I guess'd
>   at . . . .[21]

Here Whitman joins hands with Mark Twain in *The Mysterious
Stranger:*

> It was wonderful, the mastery Satan had over time and
> distance. For him they did not exist. He called them human
> inventions, and said they were artificialities.[22]

Humor thus becomes "a cosmic game between the real world
and the ideal world. [It has] the unity that comes from recognized
lack of unity," which is how Havelock Ellis defined it referring to
Heine in *The New Spirit*. This leads to cosmic visions in which
dimensions have ceased to matter:

> My ties and ballasts leave me, my elbows rest in seagaps,
> I skirt sierras, my palms cover continents. . . .[23]

The poet is turned into a sort of mystical Paul Bunyan. Lyric
poetry and the tall tale become almost identical in form—if not in
tone:

What widens within you Walt Whitman?
What waves and soil exuding?
What climes? . . .
What rivers are these? What forests and fruits are these?
What are the mountains call'd that rise so high in the
     mists? . . .
Within me latitude widens, longitude lengthens,[24]

boasts the poet. Now this is almost what Huckleberry Finn heard
the drunken raftsman shout out in the middle of the Mississippi:

> Don't attempt to look at me with the naked eye, gentlemen!
> When I'm playful I use the meridians of longitude and paral-
> lels of latitude for a seine and dry the Atlantic Ocean for
> whales! I scratch my head with the lightning and purr myself
> to sleep with the thunder. . . ." [25]

At such times, lyric poetry and humor lead to—or come from—
the same fundamental exuberance and then, just as the frontier
between the real world and the ideal world disappears, the distinc-
tions between the various layers of language are abolished. The
vernacular becomes just as legitimate as literary terms:

> Earth! you seem to look for something at my hands,
> Say, *old top-knot,* what do you want? [italics mine] [26]

Form also ceases to matter. Sprawling formlessness becomes the
rule.

As Kierkegaard noted, humor—like realism—frequently results in
prolixity. This is not surprising, for humor and realism are very
closely connected. Bergson defined humor in contradistinction
with irony as consisting in minutely and meticulously describing
things as they are while affecting to believe that they are as they
should be (i.e., in describing the real as if it were ideal).[27] "Describing things as they are" is precisely the essence of realism. So humorists often lovingly describe the physical world, as Mark Twain
does in particular in some parts of *Huckleberry Finn:*

The sun was up so high when I waked that I judged it was after eight o'clock. I laid there in the grass [a typical Whitman posture] and the cool shade, thinking about things. . . . I could see the sun out at one or two holes, but mostly it was big trees all about and gloomy in there amongst them. There was freckled places on the ground where the light sifted down through the leaves, and the freckled places swapped about a little, showing there was a little breeze up there.[28]

Whitman's eye was attracted by a similar scene, and he rendered it more concisely (but in one of his most prolix poems):

> The play of shine and shade on the trees as the supple
>   boughs wag. . . .[29]

On one occasion, Whitman's humor becomes almost uproarious when in his "Song of the Exposition" he treats the Muse with utter disrespect [30] and installs her in the middle of the kitchenware at the Fortieth Annual Exhibition in New York City—in very much the same spirit as Mark Twain treats the "Old Masters" in *Innocents Abroad.*

At other times, his humor combines with irony and bitter invective (the kind of invective he had secretly indulged in in *The Eighteenth Presidency*). He then gives full vent to his indignation and despair, as in "A Boston Ballad" and, above all, in "Respondez." He did not like this mood, however, and thought it did not match the rest of *Leaves of Grass.* He dropped "Respondez" in 1881 and kept "A Boston Ballad" only on his friend Trowbridge's insistence.

He had the true humorist's reluctance fully to commit himself and preferred to stand

> Apart from the pulling and hauling . . .
>   . . . amused, complacent, compassionating, idle, unitary . . .
> Both in and out of the game and watching and wondering at
>   it.[31]

This is an excellent description of the humorist's sympathetic and yet detached attitude toward his subject, an attitude which involves a certain amount of self-complacency and narcissism, as Freud has pointed out:

Like jokes and the comic, humour has something liberating about it; but it has also something of grandeur and elevation which is lacking in the other two ways of obtaining pleasure from intellectual activity. The grandeur in it clearly lies in the triumph of narcissism, the victorious assertion of the ego's invulnerability.[32]

It is inevitable therefore that we should find traces of humor in "Song of Myself," a "Me Myself" full of contradictions, torn between centripetal and centrifugal forces, tortured by the incongruous contrasts of the human condition, both mortal and immortal, finite and infinite, "one's-self" and "en-masse"—very much tempted at times to reach Mark Twain's despairing (and consoling) conclusion at the end of *The Mysterious Stranger:* "Life itself is only a vision, a dream." [33]

In a way, Whitman thus attained that higher form of humor which Mark Twain defined in the following way in the same book:

> The multitude see the comic side of a thousand low-grade and trivial things—incongruities, mainly; grotesqueries, absurdities, evokers of the horselaugh. The ten thousand high-grade comicalities which exist in the world are sealed to their dull vision.[34]

Among those ten thousand high-grade comicalities is man's sense of his superiority over animals. Both Whitman and Mark Twain indignantly denied it:

> They do not sweat or whine about their condition,
> They do not lie awake in the dark and weep for their sins,
> They do not make me sick discussing their duty to God,
> Not one is dissatisfied, not one is demented with the mania
>   of owning things,
> Not one kneels to another, nor to his kind that lived
>   thousands of years ago,
> Not one is respectable or unhappy over the whole earth.[35]

"It is not pleasant," says Satan in *The Mysterious Stranger* to hear you libel the higher animals by attributing to them dispositions which they are free from, and which are found nowhere but in the human heart. None of the higher animals is tainted with the disease called the Moral Sense." [36]

But, whereas at this point Mark Twain invites us to burst out laughing at man's stupidity, Whitman does no such thing. He was saved from this "descendentalism," as Carlyle would have called it, by his transcendentalism. Man in his poetry is not something to be laughed at, but, on the contrary, a miracle to be wondered at. True, we are "little plentiful mannikins skipping around in [turtleneck] collars and tail'd coats [or pullovers]," but we "are positively not worms or fleas." [37] In the last analysis, in Whitman's eyes, man is not a ludicrous and despicable biped, but an unfathomable and ungraspable mystery, "not contain'd between his hat and boots," [38] closely related to Mayakovsky's "Cloud in trousers."

A lyric poet's sense of humor cannot be quite the same as that of a prose writer and a humorist. There are as many kinds of humor as there are shades of color in the rainbow.

Notes

1. Jesse Bier, *The Rise and Fall of American Humor* (New York: Holt, Rinehart and Winston, 1968), p. 386.
2. Richard Chase, *Walt Whitman Reconsidered* (New York: William Sloane, 1955), p. 59.
3. "Farce is an extreme form of lyricism and the heroic expression of the joy of life." Quoted by Jean-Louis Barrault in "Comment fut créé le *Soulier de Satin,*" *Figaro Littéraire,* vol. VIII, no. 387, Sept. 19, 1953.
4. "Humour is wit and love." Chapter entitled "Charity and Humour" in W. M. Thackeray, *The English Humourists of the Eighteenth Century* (London: Smith, Elder 1853), p. 715.
5. " . . . Gentle reader, (we like that time-honored phrase!) . . ." in "Philosophy of Ferries" (1847) in Emory Holloway, ed., *Uncollected Poetry and Prose of Walt Whitman* (New York: Peter Smith, 1932), vol. I, p. 168.
6. "Sun-Down Papers," no. 5 (1840), ibid., p. 33.
7. "Sun-Down Papers," no. 9, ibid., p. 44.
8. Ibid., p. 133.
9. Joseph Jay Rubin and Charles H. Brown, eds., *Walt Whitman of the New York Aurora* (State College, Pa.: Bald Eagle Press, 1950), p. 52. From the *New York Aurora,* April 18, 1842.
10. "How to write a leader," ibid., p. 121.
11. Cleveland Rodgers and John Black, eds., *The Gathering of the Forces* (New York: Putnam, 1920), vol. II, pp. 272-73.

12. Horace Traubel in his introduction to Walt Whitman's *American Primer* (Boston: Small, Maynard, 1906), p. vi.

13. "Sketches of the sidewalks and levees; with glimpses into the New Orleans Bar (Rooms)," from the *Daily Crescent,* March-April 1848, in *Uncollected Poetry and Prose of Walt Whitman,* vol. I, pp. 199-216.

14. Thomas B. Harned, *Memoirs,* vol. 14, supplement 1 of *American Transcendental Quarterly* (Spring 1972), pp. 36-37.

15. Horace Traubel, *With Walt Whitman in Camden,* vol. IV, ed. by Sculley Bradley (Philadelphia: University of Pennsylvania Press, 1953), pp. 207-8.

16. Horace Traubel, *With Walt Whitman in Camden,* vol. V (Carbondale, Ill.: Southern Illinois University Press, 1964), p. 456.

17. Ibid., vol. IV, p. 208.

18. Emory Holloway, ed., *Uncollected Poetry and Prose of Walt Whitman,* vol. I, p. 72.

19. *Gathering of the Forces,* vol. II, pp. 290-91 (reprinted from the *Brooklyn Eagle,* Oct. 17, 1846).

20. Walt Whitman, *Leaves of Grass,* Comprehensive Reader's Edition, ed. by Harold W. Blodgett and Sculley Bradley (New York: W. W. Norton, 1965), "Song of Myself," paragraph 41, 11. 1026-35, p. 75. All subsequent references to *Leaves of Grass* will be to this edition, designated as *Leaves of Grass.*

21. "Song of Myself," paragraph 33, 1. 710, *Leaves of Grass,* p. 61.

22. *The Mysterious Stranger,* beginning of chapter IX, Signet Edition (London and Toronto: New American Library, 1962), p. 235.

23. "Song of Myself," paragraph 33, 11. 714-15, *Leaves of Grass,* p. 61.

24. "Salut au Monde," ll. 5-14, *Leaves of Grass,* p 137.

25. *Huckleberry Finn,* chapter XVI in the *Portable Mark Twain,* ed. by Bernard De Voto, pp. 294-95.

26. "Song of Myself," paragraph 40, 11. 989-90, *Leaves of Grass,* p. 73.

27. Henri Bergson, *Le Rire* (Paris: Alcan, 1900), pp. 130-31.

28. *Huckleberry Finn,* 1st paragraph of chap. VIII.

29. "Song of Myself," paragraph 2, 1. 27, *Leaves of Grass,* p. 30.

30. See especially the original text of the 1871 edition quoted by Emory Holloway in the Inclusive Edition of *Leaves of Grass,* p. 619.

31. "Song of Myself," paragraph 4, 11. 75-79, *Leaves of Grass,* p. 32.

32. The passage occurs in the essay entitled "Humour" in *The Standard Edition of the Complete Psychological Works of Sigmund Freud,* vol. 21, p. 162 (London: Hogarth Press, 1961).

33. *The Mysterious Stranger,* last chapter, Signet Edition, p. 252.

34. Ibid., last chapter but one, Signet Edition, p. 247.

35. "Song of Myself," paragraph 32, 11. 686-91, *Leaves of Grass,* p. 60.

36. *The Mysterious Stranger,* chapter VI, Signet Edition, p. 195. See also end of chap. V, pp. 192-93.

37. "Song of Myself," paragraph 42, 11. 1078-79, *Leaves of Grass;* p. 77.

38. "Song of Myself," paragraph 7, 1. 133, *Leaves of Grass,* p. 35.

5.

From Paumanok to India

From Paumanok to More Than America

Whoever reads the poems of Bryant, Whittier, Longfellow, Thoreau, or Emerson and then opens *Leaves of Grass* immediately realizes that there is almost a difference in kind between Walt Whitman and his predecessors.[1] Whitman's predecessors frequently tried to sing of American subjects and scenes, but their efforts always resulted in *English* poems in which they laboriously endeavored to make America look poetical. They felt that they were fighting against great odds and that they must first poeticize the unpoetic subject which they had so rashly chosen. In his essay on "The Poet," Emerson gives us the reason for their failure and for Whitman's success:

> We have yet had no genius in America, with tyrannous eye, which knew the value of our incomparable materials, and saw in the barbarism and materialism of the time another carnival of the same gods whose picture he so much admires in Homer; then in the Middle Age; then in Calvinism. Banks and tariffs,

the newspaper and caucus, Methodism and Unitarianism, are
flat and dull to dull people, but rest on the same foundations
of wonder as the town of Troy and the temple of Delphi. . . .
Our log-rolling, our stumps and their politics, our fisheries,
our Negroes and Indians, our boasts and our repudiations, the
wrath of rogues and the pusillanimity of honest men, the
northern trade, the southern planting, the western clearing,
Oregon, and Texas, are yet unsung. *Yet America is a poem in our
eyes;* its ample geography dazzles the imagination.[2]

Whitman's superiority lay in his awareness that America *was* a
poem. He repeated it again and again in *Leaves of Grass* as well as
in *Democratic Vistas:* "These States are the amplest poem," [3] "The
U.S. themselves are essentially the greatest poem." [4] In his own
words, he heard America singing:

Chants of the prairies,
Chants of the long-running Mississippi, and down to the
  Mexican sea,
Chants of Ohio, Indiana, Illinois, Iowa, Wisconsin and
  Minnesota.[5]

So, he said, "Solitary, singing in the West, I strike up for a New
World." [6]

Like the "noiseless patient spider" of his poem—and like Henry
James—he felt in the middle of a great vacant space, "in measureless oceans of space," but, instead of moving to a cluttered Victorian drawing-room like James, he decided to weave his web
where he was. Isolated, suspended in the void, "ceaselessly musing,
venturing, throwing," he "launched forth filament, filament, filament, out of [himself]" till a bridge was formed, till the gossamer
thread had caught somewhere, till he had covered with his cobweb
the great existential void which originally surrounded him. In
other words, he filled the great open spaces of the American continent with his own substance, with himself, with his dreams, and he
became one with America in the middle of his cobweb. America
was himself and he was America. "Song of Myself" is also, to a
large extent, the "Song of America," and all his poems about
America are equally about himself. Influx and efflux:

> America isolated yet embodying all, what is it finally
>   except myself?
> These States, what are they except myself?

he acknowledged in "By Blue Ontario's Shore." [7]

Leaves of Grass is both the story and the result of this identification of the poet with his country. It is not merely a great mystical poem about the sprouting of life in broad zones and in narrow zones and about the journey-work of the stars; it also records the poet's gradual discovery of America. It is a description of his journey in search of himself and of his country. As he warns us in "Song of Myself," he is both a Kosmos and an American: "I, Walt Whitman, a Kosmos, an American."

This journey of discovery started from Paumanok, that is to say, from Long Island. He deliberately preferred to call it by its Indian name, because it was a way of throwing one of his filaments further into the past. He thus renewed relations, secretly as it were, with the "strong wild race," as he says in *Democratic Vistas,* which once lived there. A similar preoccupation made him insist on the long line of Dutch, Welsh, and English settlers who had preceded him on the soil of Long Island: "Born here of parents born here from parents the same, and their parents the same," [8] he tells us at the beginning of "Song of Myself" with the same mechanical repetitiousness as the Book of Chronicles. And in *Specimen Days* he provides us with all the facts:

> The later years of the last century found the Van Velsor family, my mother's side, living on their own farm at Cold Spring, Long Island, New York State, near the eastern edge of Queens County, about a mile from the harbor. My father's side—probably the fifth generation from the first English arrivals in New England—were at the same time farmers on their own land . . . two or three miles off, at West Hills, Suffolk County. . . . John Whitman . . . came over in the True Love in 1640 to America.[9]

(Only twenty years after the Pilgrim Fathers on the *Mayflower!*) As to his mother's mother, she was a Williams and came from a family of Welsh Quakers.

Whitman dwells complacently on these "arrières of persons and scenes," as he says, to show his reader that he was well rooted in American soil. As a matter of fact he never tired of contemplating his roots. The "old pedigree reminiscences" which open *Specimen Days* were written in 1881 when he was in his sixty-third year, during a visit to West Hills and "the burial grounds of [his] ancestry, both sides." [10] And a few years later (in 1888), he composed a poem to "Old Salt Kossabone," "far back related on [his] mother's side":

> Old Salt Kossabone, I'll tell you how he died:
> (Had been a sailor all his life—was nearly 90 . . .)

and the yarn goes on.

The Whitman family was a small crucible, a melting pot, in which Dutch sailors and Welsh and English farmers, free-thinkers and Quakers had simmered for nearly two centuries before finally producing Walt Whitman. Hence his sympathy for all immigrants:

> Immigrants arriving, fifteen or twenty thousand in a
>   week, . . .[11]

> The wearied emigrants sleep, wrapt in their blankets; . . .[12]

> The groups of newly-come immigrants cover the wharf or
>   levee. . . .[13]

Actually, Whitman's glance plunged into the past much further than the coming of his family to America; it plunged from the dizzying heights of the nineteenth century, beyond prehistory, into the remote eras when the earth itself was in the making:

> I am an acme of things accomplish'd, . . .
> Immense have been the preparations for me, . . .
> Cycles ferried my cradle, rowing and rowing like cheerful
>   boatmen, . . .
> Before I was born out of my mother generations guided me,
> My embryo has never been torpid, nothing could overlay it.

For it the nebula cohered to an orb,
The long slow strata piled to rest it on,
Vast vegetables gave it sustenance,
Monstrous sauroids transported it in their mouths and
    deposited it with care.[14]
I find I incorporate gneiss, coal, long-threaded moss, fruits,
    grains, esculent roots,
And am stucco'd with quadrupeds and birds all over. . . .[15]

Thus, Walt Whitman, an American, was not contained between his hat and boots: he was indeed a Kosmos. His filaments eventually reached to the origin of things, and Paumanok was not just a "fish-shaped island" anchored off the American continent: it was part and parcel of a vast universe in a state of constant becoming. This extraordinary combination of a sense of the infinity of space with an equally vivid sense of the infinity of time is one of the originalities of Whitman's poetry.

During Walt Whitman's childhood, Long Island was certainly closer to the Stone Age than to the age of Stony Brook. It was a place where one could still loaf and take long walks and bathe on solitary beaches. There were only some seven thousand inhabitants in Brooklyn when his parents went to live there in 1823. So young Walt Whitman's life was essentially that of a country boy, as he has recalled in *Leaves of Grass:*

There was a child went forth every day. . . .
The early lilacs became part of this child
And grass and white and red morning-glories, and white and
    red clover, and the song of the phoebe-bird, . . .
And the noisy brood of the barnyard or by the mire at the
    pond-side, . . .
And the apple-trees cover'd with blossoms and the fruit
    afterward and wood-berries, . . .
The horizon's edge, the flying sea-crow, the fragrance of salt-
    marsh and shore-mud,
These became part of that child who went forth every-
    day, . . .[16]

or as he said in another poem:

> Me pleas'd, rambling in lands and country fields,
>   Paumanok's fields,
> Observing the spiral flight of two little yellow butterflies
>   shuffling between each other, ascending high in the
>   air. . . .[17]

In *Specimen Days,* which is often America-as-poem in prose, he gives more particulars:

> . . . In the middle of the island were the spreading Hempstead plains, then (1830-40) quite prairie-like, open, uninhabited, rather sterile, covered with kill-calf and huckleberry bushes, yet plenty of fair pasture for the cattle, mostly milch-cows, who fed there by hundreds, even thousands. . . . I have often been out on the edges of these plains toward sundown and can yet recall in fancy the interminable cow processions, and hear the music of the tin or copper bells clanking far or near, and breathe the cool of the sweet and slightly aromatic evening air. . . . Here, and all along the island and its shores, I spent intervals, many years, all seasons, sometimes riding, sometimes boating, but generally afoot (I have always been a good walker) absorbing fields, shores, marine incidents, the bay men, farmers, pilots, . . . went every summer on sailing trips— always liked the bare sea beach south side, and have some of my happiest hours on it to this day. . . . The shores of [Paumanok], and my doings there in early life are woven all through *L. of G.*[18]

During all those years, Whitman *absorbed* America, both passively and passionately. America became his internal world. It was not something outside himself. It was himself—that self which he was soon to sing. But he already heard America singing around him:

> I hear America singing, the varied carols I hear, . . .
> The carpenter singing his as he measures his plank or beam,
> The mason singing his as he makes ready for work, or leaves
>   off work,
> The boatman singing . . .

> The shoemaker singing as he sits on his bench, . . .
> The woodcutter's song, the ploughboy's on his way in the
>   morning. . . .[19]

America was song—and also caresses. It caressed his young body
and his body caressed it in return. He was "the caresser of life, . . .
absorbing all to [him]self and for [his] song." [20]

But soon the "caresser of life" became "the lover of populous
pavements." [21] The dreamy Long Island boy crossed Brooklyn
Ferry and discovered Manhattan and its crowds. He lived in New
York for a full year from May 1835 to May 1836—when he was
only sixteen—and he settled there as soon as he could a few years
later. He then underwent a complete metamorphosis. The country
boy now dressed like a dandy. This is how one of his friends described him: "He usually wore a frock-coat and a [top]-hat, carried
a small cane and the lapel of his coat was almost invariably orna-
mented with a boutonière," [22] He no longer thought of open
spaces; he dreamt only of walks on Broadway, of cafés and thea-
ters. He was transformed into a city man and the crowd was his
natural element. Even after he returned to Brooklyn as editor of
the *Eagle,* he took the ferry every day after work early in the afternoon and passed the rest of the day in New York, riding the Broadway omnibus seated beside the driver, gossiping familiarly with
him or declaiming verses which were lost in the noise, or observing
with untiring interest the flood of humanity on the sidewalks,
which later inspired him to write the poem "Faces." He became
the first singer of large American cities and probably the first
singer of large cities in the world.

> The blab of the pave, tires of cars, sluff of boot-soles,
>   talk of the promenaders
> The heavy omnibus, the driver with his interrogating thumb,
>   the clank of the shod horses on the granite floor.[23]

"I suppose the critics will laugh heartily," he said in *Specimen
Days,* "but the influence of those Broadway omnibus jaunts and
drivers and declamations and escapades undoubtedly entered into
the gestation of *Leaves of Grass.*" [24]

These loungings were indeed no loss of time. They enriched him, they allowed him to add to his collection of picturesque snapshots of American life, and they developed his sense of the unanimous, teeming life of a great city, of America "en-masse," as he said in his Franco-American jargon. He considered himself a "dweller in Mannahatta my city" [25] and was never so happy as "when million-footed Manhattan unpent descend[ed] to her pavements" [26] to witness "a Broadway Pageant." "Thou," he exclaimed,

> Thou of the endless sliding, mincing, shuffling feet!
> Thou portal—thou arena—thou of the myriad long-drawn
>   lines and groups! . . .
> What hurrying human tides, or day or night! [27]

And he perceived mysterious correspondences between these human tides and the tides which ceaselessly flowed and ebbed on the shores of Manhattan:

> Flow on, river! flow with the flood-tide, and
>   ebb with the ebb-tide!
> Frolic on, crested and scallop-edg'd waves! . . .
> Stand up, tall masts of Mannahatta!
> Ah, what can ever be more stately and admirable to me than
>   mast-hemm'd Manhattan! [28]

He proudly recalled the original meaning of the Indian name of Manhattan:

> *Mannahatta.*
> Choice aboriginal name, with marvellous beauty, meaning,
> *A rocky founded island—shores where ever gayly dash the coming,*
>   *going, hurrying sea waves.*[29]

He never forgot that New York was also the "City of Ships":

> City of wharves and stores . . .[30]
> Rich, hemm'd thick all around with sailships and
>   steamships, an island sixteen miles long, solid founded.[31]

But he was the poet of the body as well as the soul, so he made another discovery in New York: besides the soul of Manhattan, he discovered modern industry and did not hesitate to sing "the countless workers working in the shops" as well as the streets and piers. This was part of the "Old Feuillage" that had grown in the New World. Crossing Brooklyn Ferry at sunset, he could not help exclaiming in his enthusiasm: "Burn high your fires, foundry-chimneys! cast black shadows at nightfall! cast red and yellow light over the tops of the houses!" [32]

America thus ceased to be to him the land of lonely beaches and peaceful meadows and fields which he had known and loved as a child; it became the land of machines and factories which he adopted without the least hesitation—while all the poets of his time shrank from it and preferred to ignore it in their poems. Sidney Lanier even vituperated "the terrible towns" and "the hell-coloured smoke of the factories." True, Emerson was an exception; he had valiantly tried to bridge the gap between poetry and industry. In his essay on "The Poet" he had observed: "Readers of poetry see the factory-village and the railway, and fancy that the poetry of the landscape is broken up by these, . . . but the poet sees them fall within the great Order not less than the beehive or the spider's geometrical web." [33] But he had only timidly put into practice himself the principles which he had formulated. Whitman, on the contrary, intrepidly incorporated in his poems, from the start, the most prosaic industries and all the machines he discovered on the mainland:

> Glassblowing, nail-making, coopering, tin-roofing, . . .
> The pump, the pile-driver, the great derrick, the coal-kiln
>   and brick kiln,
> Iron works, forge-fires . . . , the sugar-house, steamsaws,
>   the great mills and factories, . . .
> Goods of gutta-percha or papier-maché, . . . electroplating,
>   electrotyping, stereotyping.[34]

All was grist that came to his poetical mill. The most technical terms were sweet music to his ear. He turned locomotives and trip hammers into poetry. He did not always succeed in transmuting them into something rich and strange, but at least he valiantly tried. So great was his enthusiasm that he kept his lists of modern inventions up to date through the successive editions of *Leaves of Grass*, adding for instance "the permutating lock, electroplating and stereotyping" as soon as they appeared, and changing "sail'd" to "steam'd" wherever he could. "Great are . . . commerce, newspapers, . . . steamers, international mails and telegraphs and exchanges," [35] he proclaimed as early as 1855, and in the open letter to Emerson which he appended to *Leaves of Grass* the next year he listed the following subjects as available to American poets: "the different trades, mechanics, . . . money, . . . free-trade, iron and the iron-mines, . . . those . . . splendid poems, the steamships of the seaboard states and those other resistless splendid poems, the locomotives. . . ." [36]

No wonder that in 1860, "the Year of Meteors," he celebrated the arrival of the *Great Eastern* in the port of New York, "well-shaped and stately, . . . 600 feet long," [37] a new wonder of the Modern World. The thought of material progress intoxicated him, and he was in raptures over the tireless dynamism of American economy. He thus fully approved of the constant wrecking of buildings which was going on in New York:

> [Take] the choicest edifices to destroy them;
> Room! room! for new far-planning draughtsmen and
>   engineers!
> Clear that rubbish from the building-spots and the paths! [38]

America to him was synonymous with perpetual change and renovation, even at the cost of destruction. He was carried away by the restless national desire for ceaselessly going further ahead.

To the end of his life he was in ecstasy before the miracles of modern technology. The organizers of the Fortieth Annual Exhibition of the American Institute in New York City were therefore well inspired when, in 1871, they invited him to read a poem at the opening ceremony. For that occasion he composed his "Song of the Exposition," which is a hymn to the glory of industry and America. In the first lines he invites the Muse to leave the Old World in order to settle in the "great cathedral" of "sacred industry" in the

United States, for the monuments and artistic treasures of Europe belong to a dead past. With its incessantly renewed creations, industry alone ought henceforth to matter in the eyes of the poets. Thus he leads his poor Muse, somewhat frightened at first by the thud of the machines and the sharp sound of the steam whistles, among the drainpipes, gasometers, and artificial fertilizers and enthrones her in the middle of pots and pans, more useful by far and closer to the realities of life than Greek or Roman temples or even "Rhenish castle-keeps." Then he takes her around the stands and spares her no detail from the harvesting of cotton to the printing of a newspaper on the marvellous Hoe press. He vaunts the latest successes of technology, the laying of the trans-Atlantic cables in particular, and exalts the infinite resources of America, the inventive mind of its inhabitants, and their innumerable patents. "The list of one week's issue of patents from the National Patent Office at Washington illustrates America and the American character about as much as anything I know," he once noted on a newspaper clipping. "What an age, what a land!" he proclaimed in *Democratic Vistas*.

Such was the revelation that he had when he left Paumanok for Manhattan, and he never got over it. He noted in the same book:

> The subject is important and will bear repetition, . . . the tumultuous streets, Broadway, the heavy, low, musical roar, hardly ever intermitted, even at night; the jobbers' houses, the rich shops, the wharves . . . —these, I say, and the like of these, completely satisfy my senses of power, fulness, motion, etc. and give me, through such senses and appetites, and through my aesthetic conscience, a continued exaltation and absolute fulfillment. I realize . . . that not Nature alone is great in her fields of freedom and the open air, . . . but in the artificial, the work of man too is equally great—in this profusion of teeming humanity—in these ingenuities, streets, goods, houses, ships— these hurrying, feverish, electric crowds of men . . . and all this mighty many-threaded wealth and industry concentrated here.[39]

He was quite as explicit in a poem which he wrote in the late 1850s:

Keep your splendid silent sun,
Keep your woods O Nature, and the quiet places by the
    woods. . . .
Give me faces and streets—give me these phantoms incessant
    and endless along the trottoirs! . . .
O such for me! O an intense life, full to repletion and
    varied!
The life of the theatre, bar-room, huge hotel, for me! . . .
Manhattan crowds, with their turbulent musical chorus!
Manhattan faces and eyes forever for me.[40]

No wonder that he once declared in a short story that "living out
of [the city] . . . was no living at all." [41] He had for his part
deliberately turned his back on the Arcadia of his childhood and
youth.

Manhattan was to him the essence and epitome of America. He
did not feel the least desire to go any further. It was only in 1848,
when he was twenty-seven, that he proceeded with his exploration
of the continent, and he then discovered New Orleans and fell in
love with the South. He "saw in Louisiana a live-oak growing,"
with moss-hung branches, "uttering joyous leaves of dark green."
"O magnet-South!" he exclaimed in another poem. On his way
there, while sailing down the Ohio and the Mississippi, he acquired that sense of the immensity and infinite potentialities of the
West which was never to leave him. But to him there was no place
like New York, and he quickly returned to his beloved Manhattan
after an absence of only four months. It took the Civil War to
make him budge again from there twelve years later. No other city
succeeded in capturing his imagination to the same extent. He
loved Washington, D.C. He celebrated in a newspaper article "the
magnificent amplitude in the laying out of the city. . . . I continually enjoy," he said, "these streets, planned on such a generous
scale, stretching far, without stop or turn, giving the eye vista. I
feel freer, larger in them. Not the squeezed limits of Boston, New
York, or even Philadelphia, but royal plenty and nature's own
bounty—American, prairie-like. . . . It is worth writing a book
about this alone," [42] he concluded, but he never wrote the book
and does not even give one line to Washington in the whole of
Leaves of Grass.

Though in 1860 he made "A Promise to California": "Sojourning east a while longer, soon I travel toward you," he never kept it. He did not travel west again until 1879, but even then he did not go beyond the Rocky Mountains—and anyway his later travels did not enrich him. On his return, he wrote only three or four insignificant pieces, including "Italian Music in Dakota" and "The Prairie States." He did not discover anything new there. What he saw merely confirmed what he had imagined. Even the Rockies failed to impress him. "Spirit that form'd this scene," he said, "I know thee, savage spirit—we have communed together." [43] " 'I have found the law of my own poems,' was the unspoken, but more and more decided feeling that came to me," he noted in his travel log after contemplating "this plenitude of material, entire absence of art, untrammeled play of primitive Nature." It was, he said, "an egotistical find." [44]

So, when he composed *Leaves of Grass*, he had only a limited experience of America. He was a tramp with "a rain-proof coat and good shoes and a staff cut in the woods" [45] in imagination only. "Allons!" he said, "Allons! . . . to undergo much, tramps of days, rests of nights." He intoned the "Song of the Open Road," but stayed at home himself. He did not have to move. He used New York as a beachhead for his imaginary sallies into the hinterland. New York was the center of his cobweb. He had been to Ohio and Louisiana. He could just as easily have gone anywhere else. So he blithely mixed up fact and fiction in his poems, as in his "Song at Sunset":

> As I steam'd down the Mississippi [which was true],
> As I wander'd over the prairies [which he did only with
>   his eyes from the deck of a Mississippi steamer], . . .
> As I bathed on the beach of the Eastern sea [true], and again
>   on the beach of the Western Sea [purely imaginary],
> As I roam'd the streets of inland Chicago [true; he went
>   there on the way back from New Orleans]. . . . [46]

One could play this game with all his poems. He boldly extrapolated his experiences and claimed that he had been everywhere. "I am the man. . . . I was there," he keeps repeating in "Song of

Myself." Actually he had not always been there. He was only recording vicarious experiences—including such a typical American experience as chasing Moby-Dick or one of his brothers:

> O the whaleman's joys! . . .
> I hear the cry again sent down from the mast-head, *There—*
> *she blows!*
> Again I spring up the rigging to look with the rest. . . .
> I leap in the lower'd boat, we row toward our prey where he
> lies.[47]

He had read books and newspaper and magazine articles about the rest of the country, so it was easy for him to imagine what life was like in Texas or Montana even though he had never set foot there. He thought for a time of preparing a special edition of *Leaves of Grass* for the West containing poems on "Wisconsin, Missouri, Texas, Lake Superior—and on the rifle"—though he had never touched one in his life. And why not? His vignettes were so vivid that his readers were taken in and believed he had really traveled everywhere. One of his earlier reviewers, Edward Everett Hale, wrote in the *North American Review:* "What he has once seen, he has seen for ever—and thus there are in this curious book little thumbnail sketches of life in the prairie, life in California, . . . life we know not where not, which as they are unfolded one after another, strike us as real." [48] Even John Burroughs, when he wrote his *Notes on Walt Whitman as Poet and Person,* believed that he had traveled through the West and Northwest of the United States.

While Walter Whitman, the man, remained most of the time in New York, Walt Whitman, the poet, thus, in his own words "roam'd many lands,"

> Starting from Paumanok,
>
> Walking New England, . . .
> Crossing the prairies, dwelling again in Chicago, dwelling in
> every town, . . .
> The Louisianan, the Georgian [near to him], . . .
> The Mississippian and Arkansian yet with [him]. . . .

On the way he drew up loving and ecstatic inventories of all the riches of America:

> Land of coal and iron! land of gold! land of cotton, sugar,
>   rice!
> Land of wheat, beef, pork! land of wool and hemp! land of
>   the apple and the grape! . . .
> Land of sierras and peaks. . . .[49]

I could in my turn draw up endless inventories of his inventories. *Leaves of Grass* in many places is a rapturous hymn to the United States:

> Here is not merely a Nation, but a teeming Nation of
>   nations,
> Here the doings of men correspond with the broadcast
>   doings of the day and night.[50]

So ardent is his patriotism that he goes so far as to proclaim: "Great is the greatest nation—the nation of clusters of equal nations!" And he added this Kiplingesque line: "It is the mother of the brood that must rule the earth with the new rule." [51]

In his enthusiasm he was quite ready for his part to annex Alaska and Canada at once, and all the islands of the Western Sea, that is to say, of the Pacific Ocean. He saw liberty diffused all over the world, thanks to the United States: "Shapes of a hundred Free States, begetting another hundred north and south . . . !" [52]

He celebrated not only the sights and sounds of the United States, but its immensity and power. There were times when he became intoxicated with large figures and tried to turn statistics into poetry:

> The area the eighty-third year of these States [i.e., 1859], the
>   three and a half millions of square miles,
> The eighteen thousand miles of sea-coast and bay-coast on
>   the main, the thirty thousand miles of river navigation,
> The seven millions of distinct families and the same number

of dwellings—always these and more, branching forth
into numberless branches.[53]

Like his ideal poet, he "incarnat[ed] the geography and natural
life and rivers and lakes" of America—not for their own sake, however, but because America was synonymous with Democracy. "I
shall use the words America and Democracy as convertible terms,"
he warns us in *Democratic Vistas,* and in 1860 he entitled a group of
poems "Chants Democratic and Native American."

Consequently, to him, the political institutions of the United
States were sheer poetry, too. He never tired of praising the Con-
stitution, "the indissoluble compact," as he called it, and elections
seemed to him just as poetical as a clambake on a Long Island
beach:

> If I should need to name, O Western World, your
>   powerfulest scene and show,
> 'Twould not be you, Niagara—nor you, ye limitless prairies—
>   nor your huge rift of canyons, Colorado, . . .
> [But] *the still small voice* vibrating—America's choosing
>   day.[54]

The "still small voice" to which he referred here was the voice of
the people which had so long been stifled in Europe, but could at
last be heard in the New World. "The good old cause," as he called
it after Milton, had eventually triumphed in America and from
then on would ceaselessly and irresistibly go forward until the
whole world was free of tyranny.

"Great is Liberty! Great is Equality!" he shouted. And he wanted
above all to sing the resistless dynamism of American democracy:

> The main shapes arise!
> Shapes of Democracy total, result of centuries,
> Shapes ever projecting other shapes,
> Shapes of turbulent manly cities. . . .[55]
>   Pioneers! O pioneers!
> For we cannot tarry here,

We must march my darlings, we must bear the brunt of
    danger,
We the youthful sinewy races, all the rest on us depend,
    Pioneers! O pioneers! [56]

This poem was written immediately after the Civil War when
the march forward could at last be resumed with renewed confidence. During the war, Whitman had left New York for Washington. The Bard of Manhattan had become "the Wound-Dresser."
After roaming the whole length and breadth of America in imagination, for nearly three years, he now traveled in depth, so to
speak, sounding the souls of the young wounded soldiers in the
military hospitals. "There have we watch'd these soldiers," he later
recorded in *Democratic Vistas,* "many of them only boys in years—
mark'd their decorum, their religious nature and fortitude and
their sweet affection. Wholesale, truly." [57] This new exploration of
America revealed to him, as "by flashes of lightning," he said, the
grandeur of average man. "Never was average man, his soul, more
energetic, more like a God. . . ." [58] he concluded. For, he said, "so
much of a race depends on how it faces death and how it stands
personal anguish and sickness." "Those three years I consider . . .
the most profound lesson of my life. . . . It has given me my most
fervent view of the true *ensemble* and extent of the *states.* " [59] The
natural heroism and spontaneous spirit of sacrifice of the average
American confirmed his faith in man en masse and in the destiny
of America.

In a way he needed this encouragement, for, side by side with
America as poem, one finds in his works, even in *Leaves of Grass,*
America as prose, anti-America, the seamy side of American democracy. For all his fervor and enthusiasm Whitman was not blind
to the defects and vices of the United States; he knew "the throes
of Democracy":

(Democracy, the destin'd conqueror, yet treacherous lip-
    smiles everywhere,
And death and infidelity at every step.) . . .
The Union always swarming with blatherers. . . . [60]

There were times when he hated the politicians who misinter-
preted the will of the people:

> They think they are providing planks of platforms on which
>   they shall stand—
> Of those planks it would be but retributive justice to make
>   them coffins.[61]

Or in another poem:

> And I will make a song for the ears of the President, full of
>   weapons with menacing points,
> And behind the weapons countless dissatisfied faces.[62]

He also often thought, he said,

> Of the President with pale face, asking secretly to himself,
>   *What will the people say at last?*
> Of the frivolous Judge—of the corrupt Congressman,
>   Governor, Mayor. . . .[63]

It saddened him, he added, to see "the swarms of cringers, suckers,
doughfaces, lice of politics, planners of sly involutions for their own
preferment to city offices, or state legislatures or the judiciary or
congress or the presidency, obtain a response of love and natural
deference from the people." [64] He fully realized what he called
"the appalling dangers of the universal suffrage in the U.S." on
account of "the people's crudeness, vice, caprices." He knew all the
tricks to which politicians resorted:

> Of the holders of public office in the Nation or the States or
> their municipalities, I have found that not one in a hundred
> has been chosen by any spontaneous selection of the outsiders,
> the people, but all have been nominated and put through by
> little or large caucuses of the politicians, and have got in by
> corrupt rings and electioneering, not capacity or desert. . . .
> And I have noticed more and more, the alarming spectacle of

parties usurping the government and openly and shamelessly wielding it for party purposes.[65]

He even wondered at times whether democracy was viable at all: "I myself see clearly enough the crude, defective streaks in all the strata of the common people, the specimens and the vast collections of the ignorant, the credulous, the unfit and uncouth, the incapable, and the very low and poor." [66] What broke his heart more than anything else was that so many people should not even believe in democracy: "Never was there perhaps more hollowness of heart than at present and here in the U.S. . . . The underlying principles of the States are not honestly believ'd in (for all this hectic glow, and these melodramatic screamings), nor is humanity itself believed in." [67]

He was also tormented by what he called "the poverty question" and "the more and more insidious grip of capital." Wasn't it a scandalous anomaly in a democratic society to have

> Many sweating, ploughing, thrashing, and then the
>   chaff for payment receiving,
> A few idly owning, and they the wheat continually
>   claiming.[68]

If the situation became worse, he felt, the social question would slowly but surely eat away the entire structure of America "like a cancer of lungs or stomach." [69]

America as prose thus debouches on nothing but chaos and despair, but Whitman agonistes, the teacher of athletes, did not acknowledge himself defeated so easily. He instinctively believed in Hegelian dialectics, and this clash between the America of his dreams and the anti-America of his experience resulted only in the vision of a super-America whose coming he prophesied throughout *Leaves of Grass.* On the disappointing and imperfect America of the present he superimposed the perfect America of the future: "The morbid facts of American politics and society everywhere are but passing incidents and flanges of our unbounded impetus of growth —weeds, annuals of the rank, rich soil—not central, enduring, perennial things." [70] Being a poet, he equated comparison with reason and later found a wonderful analogy to justify his faith. In a poem entitled "Wandering at Morn" he compared America to a thrush feeding on filthy worms, but transforming them into songs of ecstatic joy. In the same way, he thought, the United States would also some day transmute all the meannesses and scandals which it lived on into harmony and beauty:

> If worms, snakes, loathsome grubs, may to sweet spiritual
>   songs be turn'd,
> If vermin so transposed, so used and bless'd may be,
> Then may I trust in you, your fortunes, days, my coun-
>   try; . . .
> From these your future song may rise with joyous trills,
> Destin'd to fill the world.[71]

He used the same kind of comparison in *Democratic Vistas:* "Nature's stomach is fully strong enough, not only to digest the morbific matter always presented, not to be turn'd aside, . . . but even to change such contributions into nutriment for highest use and life." [72]

As he believed in perpetual progress and was endowed with a strong sense of the becoming, he generally resorted to still another image, that of a journey—a journey through space and time toward the ideal America of the future. The titles of most of his longer poems suggest a departure and some form of travel: "Starting from Paumanok," "Song of the Open Road," "Crossing Brooklyn Ferry," "A Song of the Rolling Earth," "Aboard at a Ship's Helm," "Patroling Barnegat," "Passage to India." He even called a whole section of *Leaves of Grass* "Songs of Parting."

From the beginning to the end of his poetical career, he was haunted by the image of Columbus leaving the Old World for the New. He had mentioned him even before *Leaves of Grass,* in *Pictures* in the early 1850s, and devoted to him the very last poem that he wrote a few days before his death: "A Thought of Columbus." It was Columbus, he thought, who gave America its meaning and purpose. Thanks to Columbus,

> The rapid cumulus—trade, navigation, war, peace,
>   democracy, roll on; . . .
> The tangled, long-deferr'd éclaircissement of human life and
>   hopes boldly begins untying,
> As here to-day up-grows the Western World.[73]

In the "Prayer of Columbus" which he wrote after being struck with paralysis in 1873, he wholly identified himself with Columbus "old, poor and paralyzed" (Columbus never was paralyzed) and represented him as the prophet of a better world and the discoverer not only of actual America but of the America of the future:

> Is it the prophet's thought I speak, or am I raving? . . .
> I know not even my own work past or present,
> Dim, ever-shifting guesses of it spread before me,
> Of newer, better worlds, their mighty parturition,
> Mocking me, perplexing me. . . .
> As if some miracle, some hand divine unseal'd my eyes,
> Shadowy, vast shapes smile through the air and sky. . . .[74]

And Whitman, who regarded himself as Columbus's successor in the relay race of history, proclaimed:

> A special song before I go I'd sing . . .
> For thee, the future.
> Belief I sing, and preparation;
> As Life and Nature are not great with reference to the
>   present only,
> But greater still from what is yet to come.[75]

And the dying redwood tree on the Western shore echoed his prophecy:

> I see the genius of the modern, child of the real and ideal,
> Clearing the ground for broad humanity, the true America,
>   heir of the past so grand,
> To build a grander future.[76]

"America is prophecy," Whitman acknowledged in his 1876 preface to *Leaves of Grass*. In a way, he could have said: "America is not, but will be." In order to escape the despairing vision of America as prose, he had to transcend the present and dematerialize the United States, leaving far behind real America and soaring toward the *Real*, that is to say, toward what *we* call the *Ideal*. The namer turned seer. Present-day America is "surely going somewhere," he felt, and it seemed to him that at the end of the Democratic Vistas which he had explored in his little political treatise he could catch a glimpse of the Ideal City of the Future: Real America,

> And thou America, . . .
> Thou too surroundest all,
> Embracing carrying welcoming all, thou too by pathways
>   broad and new,
> To the ideal tendest.[77]

America as prose, anti-America, is thus finally denied and abolished. We leave the plane of accidents and mere existence to reach the plane of essences. America ceases to be a land and becomes an Idea, "the great Idea."

> In spiral routes, by long detours,
> (As a much-tacking ship upon the sea,)
> For it the partial to the permanent flowing,
> For it the real to the ideal tends.[78]

As another poem shows, this "much-tacking ship" is the

> Ship of the World—Ship of Humanity—Ship of the ages—
>   Ship that circles the world,
> Ship of the hope of the world—Ship of Promise,[79]

which is tantamount to saying that America in this culminating apotheosis is a metaphor for the whole of mankind or for the future of the human race. America then completely evaporates. It is no longer a well-defined place. It becomes a dream out of space and out of time, a marvellous new mode of life which will enable all men to forget "ostensible realities," "material comforts" and problems, which will allow all men at last to fulfill themselves and acquire individual souls (if they do not have any yet):

> But behold! such [ostensible realities] swiftly subside, burnt
>   up for religion's sake, . . .
> I say that the real and permanent grandeur of these States
>   must be their religion,
> Otherwise there is no real and permanent grandeur.[80]

Just as America is Democracy, the culmination of mankind's history, the culmination of America and Democracy is the soul—the soul of each individual:

> Thou Mother with thy equal brood,
> . . . thou shalt face thy fortunes, thy diseases, and surmount
>   them all, . . .
> They each and all shall lift and pass away and cease from
>   thee,
> While thou, Time's spirals rounding, out of thyself, thyself
>   still extricating, fusing . . .
> Shalt soar toward the fulfilment of the future . . .
> The soul its destinies.

> The soul its destinies, the real real
> (Purport of all these apparitions of the real;)
> In thee America, the soul, its destinies,
> Thou globe of globes! thou wonder nebulous! [81]

At this point, Whitman had indeed traveled a long way in his journey of discovery: after "Starting from Paumanok," "Crossing Brooklyn Ferry," settling in Manhattan, exploring in person or in imagination the whole of America, he had finally embarked on a passage to more than America.

To More than India

"Passage to India" was not Whitman's swan-song, as it has sometimes been called (the description would suit "The Prayer of Columbus" much better), but rather his ode to a skylark, his most ethereal verse, in which his soul took its flight and soared to the infinite, leaving far behind its inseparable companion until then, the "excrementitious body, to be burn'd, or render'd to powder, or buried" ("A Song of Joys," l. 141). "Passage to India" is the highest and purest expression of Whitman's mystical spiritualism, and as such it is better understood nowadays in the land of "budding bibles" than in America. In the United States, on the contrary, scholars tend to run it down. Edwin Haviland Miller, in an otherwise searching book on *Walt Whitman's Poetry,* considers it the work "of a poet in retreat both in his art and his subject matter." And he adds: "The poem consists of shreds and patches from earlier motifs and lines which his art cannot successfully fuse into a new variation upon old subject matter" (p. 213). This is definitely unfair. Miller even goes so far as to object to Whitman's frequent use of exclamation points, "which may overwhelm the eye but scarcely convinces the mind" (p. 216), as if it were not the essence of a poem to be an exclamation mark followed by a ripple of points of suspension. He also criticizes Whitman's description of mankind as

> Wandering, yearning, curious, with restless explorations,
> With questionings, baffled, formless, feverish, with never
>   happy hearts,
> With that sad incessant refrain, *Wherefore unsatisfied soul?* and
>   *Whither O mocking life?*

This, he says, is "a picture of the human race alienated from nature and love," a portrait of man as a "neurotic" creature. Now it is my contention that this is, on the contrary, a true picture of man, and there is nothing neurotic whatever about asking oneself what the meaning of life and death is. This is precisely what gives man his dignity and distinguishes him from animals which neither laugh nor weep, but only grunt and bear it. He knows that he is mortal and understandably worries and frets about his condition and keeps asking such questions as: What is life? What is death? What is grass? And the whole volume of *Leaves of Grass* is an attempt to answer these questions, and "Passage to India" in particular is an effort to reach a serene conclusion after many "agonistic throes" ("A Song of Joys," l. 130). It is still as valid today as when Whitman wrote it, since the problem has not changed and there is still the same hiatus between material and spiritual progress as in his time. The hiatus even tends to become deeper.

Whitman was moved to write "Passage to India" by the rapid succession of three great events: the successful laying of a trans-Atlantic cable, the opening of the Suez canal, and the joining of the Union Pacific and Central Pacific railroad tracks in Utah. All this meant faster communication between East and West. It seemed to Whitman that mankind had now come full circle. Man had been born in Asia in the Garden of Eden, had ever since traveled restlessly westward, discovered America, and now was in a position to return to Asia, the cradle of the race. The history of mankind was thus in a way a "Passage to India." But the poem was not meant merely to celebrate the achievements of modern technology. It marked a new orientation in Whitman's thought, which he thus defined in *Two Rivulets:* "It was originally my intention after chanting in *Leaves of Grass* the songs of the Body and Existence, to then compose a further, equally needed volume, based on those convictions of perpetuity and conservation which . . . make the unseen Soul govern absolutely at last." In other words, he proposed in "Passage to India" to sing the soul above all. So the poem is also a "passage to more than India," a hymn to that Spirit hidden behind material appearances, which Asia at a very early date sang in its "deep diving bibles and legends."

"Passage to India" is thus an attempt at a synthesis along Hegelian lines of the mysticism of the past and the scientific achievements of the present. The result is to be a "worship new" whose high priest will be "the poet worthy of that name."

Besides summing up the history of mankind, the poem can be regarded as describing Whitman's own spiritual itinerary. It suggests the return of the poet's soul to its divine source after it has left behind the body's gross appetites. It expresses his unquenched mystical thirst and his joyful belief in his eventual reunion with God, the "Comrade perfect."

"Passage to India" is, above all, the fervent expression of a deep-seated religious faith. So to anyone who does not have at least one ounce of religious sense, it will always remain a dead letter. A psychoanalytical reading of it will bring to the surface only the standard answers: nostalgia of the maternal womb, death wish, etc. (as if the unconscious of man contained nothing but sexual drives and sex were an end in itself, not a means to other ends), and will miss the essential meaning, the meaning which Whitman deliberately chose to convey. There is no point in trying to X-ray the poem for hidden motives; it must be read for what it is, for what Whitman wanted it to be.

The Passage to India of which he dreamt a hundred years ago has not been completed yet as far as the history of mankind is concerned. The synthesis of East and West, of spiritualism and materialism has not been achieved. But there is no reason for giving up hope. The way to individual salvation is still open to each of us. It is up to us to follow the path indicated by Whitman and to take immediate passage to more than India.

Notes

1. This paper was read at the State University of New York at Albany on April 26, 1968, as part of a discussion sponsored by the Department of English on "America as Poem."
2. R. W. Emerson, *Essays,* 2nd Series (Boston: Houghton, Mifflin, 1899), pp. 40-41.
3. "By Blue Ontario's Shore," l. 60, in *Leaves of Grass,* Comprehensive Reader's Edition, ed. by Harold W. Blodgett and Sculley Bradley (New York: W. W. Norton, 1965). This edition is used throughout this chapter; further references are cited by title and line or page numbers.
4. Ll. 12-13 of the 1855 Preface to *Leaves of Grass.*
5. "Starting from Paumanok," ll. 40-42.
6. Ibid., l. 14.
7. "By Blue Ontario's Shore," ll. 309-10.
8. "Song of Myself," l. 7.
9. "Genealogy—Van Velsor and Whitman," in *Specimen Days,* foreword by Richard Chase (New York: New American Library of World Literature, 1961), pp. 19-20.

10. Idem.
11. "Mannahatta," l. 12.
12. "Night on the Prairies," l. 3.
13. "Song of Myself," l. 285.
14. Ibid., ll. 1147, 1157, 1159, 1162-66.
15. Ibid., ll. 670-71.
16. "There Was a Child Went Forth," ll. 1, 5-6, 8, 13, 38-39.
17. "Our Old Feuillage," ll. 55-56.
18. "Paumanok and My Life on It as Child and Young Man," *Specimen Days,* pp. 25-26.
19. "I Hear America Singing," ll. 1, 3, 7.
20. "Song of Myself," ll. 232, 234.
21. "Starting from Paumanok," l. 3.
22. Quoted by Bliss Perry, *Walt Whitman* (Boston and New York: Houghton Mifflin, 1906), pp. 22-23.
23. "Song of Myself," ll. 154-55.
24. "Omnibus Jaunts and Drives," *Specimen Days,* p. 32.
25. "Starting from Paumanok," l. 4.
26. "A Broadway Pageant," l. 9.
27. "Broadway," ll. 9, 6, 1.
28. "Crossing Brooklyn Ferry," ll. 101-2, 105, 92.
29. "Mannahatta," ll. 2-3.
30. "City of Ships," l. 8.
31. "Mannahatta," l. 6.
32. "Crossing Brooklyn Ferry," l. 121.
33. R. W. Emerson, *Essays,* 2nd Series (Boston: Houghton, Mifflin, 1899), p. 23.
34. "A Song for Occupations," ll. 104, 106-7, 108-10, 115, 119.
35. *Leaves of Grass* (1855), p. 95.
36. "Prefatory Letter to Ralph Waldo Emerson," pp. 736-37.
37. "Year of Meteors," l. 15.
38. "So Long!" *Leaves of Grass,* ed. Emory Holloway, Inclusive Edition (New York: Doubleday, Doran, 1927), p. 703, ll. 7-9 in the passage which originally followed l. 14 in 1860.
39. Malcolm Cowley, ed., *The Complete Poetry and Prose of Walt Whitman* (New York: Pellegrini and Cudahy, 1948), II, 215.
40. "Give Me the Splendid Silent Sun," ll. 20-21, 24, 32-33, 39-40.
41. "The Shadow and the Light of a Young Man's Soul," *Uncollected Poetry and Prose,* ed. by Emory Holloway (Garden City, N.Y.: Doubleday, Page, 1921), vol. I, 229.
42. Ibid., vol. II, 29.
43. "Spirit That Form'd This Scene," ll. 1, 6.
44. "An Egotistical 'Find,' " *Specimen Days,* p. 194.
45. "Song of Myself," l. 1203.
46. "Song at Sunset," ll. 45-46, 49-50.
47. "A Song of Joys," ll. 73-77.

48. Quoted by Roger Asselineau, *The Evolution of Walt Whitman* (Cambridge, Mass.: Harvard University Press, 1962), vol. II, p. 327, n. 37.
49. "Starting from Paumanok," ll. 1, 213, 215, 219-20, 195-96, 203.
50. "By Blue Ontario's Shore," ll. 61-62.
51. "Great Are the Myths," ll. 29, 46.
52. "Song of the Broad-Axe," Inclusive Edition, p. 617.
53. "Our Old Feuillage," ll. 5-7.
54. "Election Day, November, 1884," ll. 1-2, 5.
55. "Song of the Broad Axe," ll. 249-254.
56. "Pioneers! O Pioneers!" ll. 4-8.
57. *Complete Poetry and Prose,* vol. II, 220.
58. "Years of the Modern," l. 15.
59. "Three Years Summ'd Up," *Specimen Days,* p. 109.
60. "By Blue Ontario's Shore," ll. 7-8, 90.
61. "Of the Democratic Party 58-59-60."
62. "Starting from Paumanok," ll. 76-77.
63. "Thoughts," ll. 3-4.
64. "Preface to 1855 Edition," p. 721.
65. "Democratic Vistas," *Complete Poetry and Prose,* vol. II, p. 227.
66. Ibid., p. 221.
67. Ibid., p. 214.
68. "Song of Myself," ll. 1073-74.
69. "Democratic Vistas," *Complete Poetry and Prose,* vol. II, 233.
70. Preface to the 1876 Edition, p. 748.
71. "Wandering at Morn," ll. 9-11, 13-14.
72. *Complete Poetry and Prose,* vol. II, 224.
73. "A Thought of Columbus," ll. 15-17.
74. "Prayer of Columbus," ll. 58-61, 63-64
75. "Thou Mother with Thy Equal Brood," ll. 3-4, 10-12.
76. "Song of the Redwood-Tree," ll. 163-5.
77. "Song of the Universal," ll. 42, 45-47.
78. Ibid., ll. 16-19.
79. "Ship of Libertad," ll. 19-22.
80. "Starting from Paumanok," ll. 119, 110-11.
81. "Thou Mother with Thy Equal Brood," ll. 1, 116, 118-19, 121-26.

6.

Whitman: A Poet Both
Born and Made

Walt Whitman probably read Taine's *History of English Literature* shortly after it became available in an English translation in the United States in 1871, while he was working as a clerk in the Department of Justice in Washington. He could then borrow all the books he wanted from the library of the department, and read them at night in his office after working hours in the light of that "splendid astral lamp" which he described in such glowing terms in a letter to his mother. He was apparently so struck by Taine's theories that he prepared a long review of the History of English Literature, taking up twenty pages of blank stationery of the Department of Justice. This review was never published in his lifetime, but the manuscript has survived and is now in the Charles E. Feinberg Walt Whitman Collection in the Library of Congress.

It is essentially a summary of Taine's book which often merely paraphrases or even literally reproduces entire passages of the original. Yet, though mainly a compilation, it is interesting and important because it shows that Whitman paid particular attention to Taine's method and fully realized all its implications.

First, Whitman was well aware of Taine's debt to Sainte-Beuve with regard to the treatment of individual authors. "This is the first *elaborated* History, comprehending many centuries of a concrete and consecutive National Literature written according to the school of modern criticism born in France of Ste Beuve," he pointed out in the very first paragraph of his review. And later he added:

> When Taine would fully represent a poet, Shakespeare, Dryden, Byron, he not only presents his age, public events, excitements, etc., but the poet's parentage, sometimes even his aunts and uncles, always his inherited peculiarities, physical facts, places, personal manners, and as much as possible of everything about him, education, atmosphere, religion, and the like, affecting and permeating him.[3]

Whitman could only subscribe to such principles as applied so well to his own case, he felt, and confirmed his own impressions. He knew that his poetical personality had to a large extent been shaped by his surroundings and by family influences during his childhood. He had already expressed it lyrically in "There Was a Child Went Forth" and in some passages of "Song of Myself." At the beginning of "Song of Myself" he even proclaimed:

> My tongue, every atom of my blood, form'd from this soil,
>   this air,
> Born here of parents born here from parents born the same
>   and their parents the same.

"Any book is biographical—even autobiographical," he declared to Traubel in his old age, and he was certainly thinking of *Leaves of Grass* when he said so.[4] But Sainte-Beuve's method encouraged him to go beyond the implicit and indirect expression of his "self" in his poems. It was probably as a direct application of these principles that he devoted so many pages of *Specimen Days* to his "Genealogy" and "Two Old Family Interiors" and to the Brooklyn and New York of his childhood and youth. He now wanted to show in detail that his genius was the product of his ancestry and environment and *Specimen Days* was meant to be an autobiography "in clear," giving the reader a code with which to decipher the secret autobiography underlying *Leaves of Grass.* It was in a way a piece of biographical criticism and the equivalent of one of Sainte-Beuve's "portraits," or of a chapter in Taine's *History of English Literature.* The influence of these two critics probably also explains why Whitman insisted on writing, himself, "the account of [his] birthplace and antecedents which occupies the first twenty four pages," [5] as he admitted himself, of the *Walt Whitman* published by Richard Maurice Bucke in 1883, whereas he had been much more reticent when John Burroughs worked at his *Notes on Walt Whitman as Poet and Person* in 1867, though he wrote part of the book himself and revised the rest.

In his review of the *History of English Literature,* Whitman also defined with great clarity Taine's own contribution to French criticism, namely his historical method, which resulted from an extension and a systematization of Sainte-Beuve's theories. According to Taine, he wrote

> With respect to the past, a book, a poem, a religious treatise, a code of laws, is as the mould, the shell, left by an animal which itself has lived and perished. The animal under and behind that shell, the poem, the book, was *Man.* You must study the shell to find out what kind of man. You do not investigate in it an isolated thing, a mere abstract curiosity or beautiful object, to be judged by itself, but in reference to its antecedents, and in connection with place, time, the race, the surroundings, the epoch. Only in such amplitude of ever expanding radiations and references do you get at any fine literary production's real character and meaning.[6]

This attempt at explaining literary works by the interplay of three determining factors: race, place, and time, moved Whitman to enthusiasm. In his eyes, Taine's predecessors had been at best "first class tailors or milliners," while Taine himself was "a first class anatomist or sculptor" [7] with a full understanding of what the body of a nation's literature really was. The reason he approved so warmly was that there was a preestablished harmony between

Taine's views and his own. Whitman also believed in the importance of the racial factor. He said so in *Democratic Vistas:*

> Subtly interwoven with the materiality and personality of a
> land, a race—Teuton, Turk, Californian, or what not—there is
> always something. I can hardly tell what it is—history but
> describes the results of it—it is the same as the untellable look
> of some human faces.[8]

Beside, he was fully convinced that *Leaves of Grass* faithfully reflected both his time and his land. Glancing over traveled roads in
1888, he wrote:

> I know very well that my "Leaves" could not possibly have
> emerged or been fashion'd or completed from any other era
> than the latter half of the Nineteenth century, nor any other
> land than democratic America, and from the absolute tri
> umph of the National Union Arms.[9]

A further reason for Whitman's approval of Taine's views on
literary history was that he thought that the *History of English Literature* contained "A Lesson for America" (and he intended to use
this phrase as a title for his review). For, if race, time, and place
had gradually shaped a national literature in England, why should
not the same phenomenon take place in America? Again and again
in the *Brooklyn Eagle* he had expressed his conviction that an "Independent American Literature," a "Home Literature," [10] as he
called it, would necessarily soon appear in the United States. The
problem of the birth and growth of a native literature obsessed
him. He returned to it in *Democratic Vistas* and, toward the end of
his life, in a brief piece entitled "American National Literature,"
he still asked—rather stridently: "American National Literature—is
there distinctively any such thing, or can there ever be?" [11] He was
all the more insistent because it was both a national and a personal
problem. He had a stake in it. *Leaves of Grass* had been an attempt
to create a specifically American poem. He pointed it out in the
Preface in 1876:

Estimating the American Union as so far and for some time in its yet formative condition, I therefore now bequeath my Poems and Essays as nutriment and influences to help truly assimilate and harden and especially to furnish something toward what the States most need of all, and which seems to me yet quite unsupplied in literature, namely, to show them, Themselves distinctively, and what They are for.[12]

In the 1870s, whether because of Taine's *History of English Literature* or not, he was full of hope. For, if England had assimilated French literature and, after slavishly imitating it, had eventually transcended it and developed a vigorously original literature of her own, there was no reason why economic and territorial expansion should not have the same stimulating effects in America as in Elizabethan England: "This opening," wrote Whitman, commenting on Taine's chapter on the Renaissance, "has certain philosophical statements, suggestions specially needed for the United States." [13]

But at the end of his life he did not feel so sanguine about the future. All the conditions necessary for the development of a great literature set forth by Taine had been realized, and yet no great American literature was forthcoming: "the high pitched taunt of Margaret Fuller, forty years ago," he despaired, "still sounds in the air: 'It does not follow, because the United States print and read more books, magazines and newspapers than all the rest of the world, that they have therefore a literature.' " [14] Apparently the connection between cause and effect worked out by Taine was not always operative, and this failure may have dampened Whitman's enthusiasm.

Anyway, in the last analysis, there could be no complete agreement between Whitman and Taine, for Whitman always saw the two opposite sides of a question. In his *History of English Literature* Taine had laid emphasis on the group, on the nation, while Whitman could not accept such onesidedness. On the literary as well as on the political plane he had to balance the requirements of society by the rights of the individual. He never resigned himself completely to merging his individuality, his "identity," as he called it, either in God or in his fellow citizens *en masse*. Though as an American and a champion of democracy he clamored for a national literature and accepted Taine's theory of literary history, as a poet he again and again stressed the supreme importance of the self—"Myself," "One's Self." "Always a knit of identity, always distinction" (as opposed to fusion), he exclaimed in "Song of Myself." [15] He insisted on the fundamental isolation of each individual, "the pride and centripetal isolation of a human being in himself—identity—personalism," [16] and he added: "Alone and identity, and the mood—and the soul emerges, and all statements, churches, sermons melt away like vapors." [17] The "singer solitary" [18] could not accept the idea of being reduced to one item among others in some *History of American Literature* written by a Taine of the future.

Moreover, Whitman could not agree with Taine that the "invisible man," as Taine called him, was submitted to the determinism of sociology and psychology just as the "visible man" was submitted to the determinism of physical laws. In his review, he dropped and ignored all this aspect of Taine's introduction to the *History of English Literature*.[19] Like the romantics, like Carlyle in particular, he believed for his part in the primacy and independence of genius:

> though it may not be realized, it is strictly true that a few first-class poets, philosophers, and authors, have substantially settled and given status to the entire religion, education, law, sociology, etc., of the hitherto civilized world by *tinging and often creating the atmosphere out of* which they have arisen. [Italics mine.] [20]

His position then was the very reverse of that of Taine. According to him, great men modify their environment instead of being modified by it. Poe, for instance, far from being shaped by his "antecedents . . . his so-call'd education," grew "often, very often, in a strange spurning of, and reaction from," the places and circumstances in which he happened to find himself.[21] As for Shakespeare and George Fox, "strange as it may sound," Whitman noted, "[they] were born and bred of similar stock, in much the same surroundings and station in life—from the same England—and at a similar period." [22] So Taine's laws did not apply here. The three factors (race, time, and place) cannot account for and still less explain away the miracle of genius. If Taine's theories were true, why did not any of his brothers write *Leaves of Grass* in his stead? What really matters ultimately is not the geographical and historical context but the spark which ignites the whole, and literary history, Whitman realized, was powerless to explain such a phenomenon. No history of literature can satisfactorily describe the growth of a writer. "The process," Whitman pointed out, "is indirect and peculiar, and though it may be suggested cannot be defined." [23] There always remains a core of mystery, an indivisible atom, which the writer himself cannot explain: "There is that in me—I do not know what it is—but I know it is in me . . . ," Whitman wrote in "Song of Myself." [24] "The efflux of the soul comes from within through embower'd gates, ever provoking questions," he added in "Song of the Open Road." [25]

Though no romantic, André Gide, who was both a creator and a critic, was keenly aware of this "divine magic of . . . genius," as Whitman called it,[26] and commented upon it in his *Journal*, using, by a strange coincidence, the very example of Whitman:

> There are poets, who, as it seems, could have written their works anyhow, anywhere (and however ignorant of the works of others they might have been). I do realize that a Whitman, for instance, could not have been born elsewhere than in America, but what I mean is that, once born, he would have written his *Leaves of Grass* in any country or period.[27]

Walt Whitman must have felt this intensely too, for whenever he wrote critical essays, instead of underlining racial or historical resemblances like Taine, he tried on the contrary, like Sainte-Beuve, to bring out the fundamental differences, irreducible idiosyncrasies.[28] He attempted to define that undefinable quality which, for example, made such diverse writers as Poe and Carlyle write what they did rather than something else. And the result was a series of remarkably searching thumbnail sketches scattered all over *Specimen Days, November Boughs,* and *Good-Bye My Fancy,* in which, with admirable insight, fairness, and sympathy, much as they differed from him, he analyzed in turn Emerson, Longfellow, Whittier, Burns, Tennyson, Shakespeare, and others.[29] For all his praises of

Taine's historical approach, being a poet, he finally preferred the "natural or physiological criticism of Sainte-Beuve" [30] as more in harmony with his "Song of Myself."

Notes

1. Letter to his mother dated March 12, 1867, *Collected Writings of Walt Whitman* (New York: New York University Press, 1961), vol. I of the Correspondence, p. 318.
2. See *A Selection of the Manuscripts, Books and Association Items gathered by Charles E. Feinberg* (Detroit, Mich., 1955), pp. 12-13. This review was published for the first time with an Introduction and Notes by Roger Asselineau under the title "Un inédit de Walt Whitman: Taine's *History of English Literature*" in *Etudes Anglaises*, vol. X, no. 2, pp. 128-38 (avril-juin 1957).
3. *Etudes Anglaises*, vol. X, 135 (avril-juin 1957).
4. Traubel, p. 452.
5. Edward Carpenter, *Days with Walt Whitman* (London: Allen, 1906), p. 37.
6. *Etudes Anglaises*, vol. X, pp. 136-37.
7. Democratic Vistas (1871) in *Complete Poetry and Prose of Walt Whitman*, ed. Malcolm Cowley (New York: Pellegrini and Cudahy, 1948), vol. II, p. 248. See also "No great poem or other literary or artistic work of any scope, old or new, can be essentially consider'd without weighing first the age, politics (or want of politics) . . . out of the midst of which it rises and is formulated. . . ." "An Old Man's Rejoinder," ibid., p. 492.
8. Ibid., p. 248.
9. "A Backward Glance O'er Travel'd Roads," *Leaves of Grass*, Inclusive Ed., p. 526. See also: ". . . Herder taught to the young Goethe that really great poetry is always (like the Homeric or Biblical canticles) the result of a national spirit. . . ." Ibid., p. 536.
10. *Gathering of the Forces*, vol. II, pp. 237-45.
11. *Complete Poetry and Prose*, vol. II, p. 500.
12. Preface to 1876 Edition, Inclusive Ed. of *Leaves of Grass*, p 519.
13. *Etudes Anglaises*, vol. X, p. 133.
14. "American National Literature," *Complete Poetry and Prose*, vol. II, p. 503.
15. Sec. 28, l. 1.
16. "Democratic Vistas," in *Complete Poetry and Prose*, vol. II, p. 231.
17. Ibid., p. 236.
18. "Out of the Cradle Endlessly Rocking," l. 150.
19. True, in "A Backward Glance O'er Travel'd Roads," he quoted Taine as saying that: "All original art is self-regulated, and no original art can be regulated from without; it carries its own counterpoise, and does not receive it from elsewhere—lives on its own blood." (*Leaves of Grass*, Inclusive Ed., p. 535.) But Whitman wrenched the passage from its deterministic context.
20. "Democratic Vistas," *Complete Poetry and Prose*, vol. II, p. 211.

21. "Edgar Poe's Significance," in "Specimen Days," ibid., p. 157.
22. "George Fox (& Shakspere)," in "November Boughs," ibid., p. 491.
23. "Democratic Vistas," ibid., p. 253.
24. Sec. 50, l. 1. See also: "In the midst of all [*Leaves of Grass*] gives one man's—the author's—identity, ardors, observations, faiths, and thoughts, color'd hardly at all with any decided coloring from other faiths and other identities." "A Backward Glance O'er Travel'd Roads," *Leaves of Grass,* Inclusive Ed., p. 524.
25. Sec. 7, l. 2.
26. See note 23.
27. "Il est certains poètes . . . qui, semble-t-il, eussent écrit tout de même leur oeuvre en quelque temps qu'ils fussent nés (et quelle que soit leur ignorance de la littérature d'autrui). Je sens très bien qu'un Whitman, par exemple, ne pouvait naître qu'Américain, mais je veux dire qu'une fois né, il eût écrit n'importe où et n'importe quand ses Brins d'herbe. . ." (*Journal,* Pléiade Ed., vol. I, p. 723).

    George Santayana expressed much the same idea: "In the past or in the future, my language and my borrowed knowledge would have been different, but under whatever sky I had been born, I should have had the same philosophy." Quoted by Newton P. Stallknecht in *George Santayana,* University of Minnesota Pamphlet, 1972, p. 19.
28. Cf. T. S. Eliot in his essay "Tradition and the Individual Talent": "One of the facts that might come to light in this process is our tendency to insist, when we praise a poet, upon those aspects of his work in which he least resembles anyone else. In these aspects or parts of his work we pretend to find what is individual, what is the peculiar essence of the man." *Selected Essays (1917-1932)* (London: Faber & Faber, 1934), p. 14.
29. The five volumes of *With Walt Whitman in Camden* contain innumerable such sketches carefully recorded by Horace Traubel. The discussion of Sidney Lanier, for instance, in vol. I, pp. 170-71, is particularly remarkable.
30. Sainte-Beuve used these very words to describe his own method in *Nouveaux lundis,* vol. IX, p. 70.

7.

Theodore Dreiser's Transcendentalism

Historians of literature unanimously regard Theodore Dreiser as a naturalistic novelist. This, however, is a very hasty conclusion. If astronomers also judged by appearances, they would maintain that the moon is nothing but a flat disk hanging in the sky or a hemisphere unaccountably cut off from its other half. Dreiser, like the moon, is composed of two hemispheres, one which meets the eye, his naturalism; the other which generally remains in the dark and which only a few bold critics like Alfred Kazin, F. O. Matthiessen, and Charles Walcutt have ventured to explore,[1] namely his transcendentalism. At first sight, the two notions may seen incompatible. Yet, Dreiser somehow managed to reconcile them. Like a true transcendentalist he was indifferent to contradictions and cared little for logic.[2] He felt that, since life was made up of contraries, he had the right to include them side by side in his mind.

There are those, he wrote in *A Traveler at Forty*, who still think that life is something which can be put into a mold and adjusted to a theory, but I am not one of them. I cannot view life or human nature save as an expression of contraries—in

99

fact I think that is what life is. I know there can be no sense of heat without cold; no fulness without emptiness; no force without resistance; no anything, in short, without its contrary.[3]

Consequently he saw no inconsistency in describing psychological and social phenomena from a materialistic standpoint with the detachment—and sometimes the jargon—of a scientist, while at the same time expressing the wonder of a child or poet before the mystery of life. He constantly swung between these two extreme positions and the amplitude of the oscillation increased to such an extent in the last few months of his life that he was eventually both a fervent religionist and a member of the Communist Party. But he did not mind being in uncertainties. He confessed it in *A History of Myself*: "Chronically nebulous, doubting, uncertain, I stared and stared at everything, only wondering, not solving." So, on his own admission, he never reached any intellectual certainty. His mind restlessly groped for some transcendent reality beyond material appearances, for something which the meshes of scientific laws failed to catch—in short, he was a transcendentalist first and foremost.

Dreiser's transcendentalism is most forcibly expressed in a much-neglected collection of poems in free verse which he very fittingly entitled *Moods*.[4] According to his own testimony it was "written between 1914 and 1926" [5] and he kept revising and enlarging it for another ten years, which shows how much he prized it. In his own words, it "represents in the first instance a fair summary of [his] philosophy in mood form, and in the second, an elaborated presentation of it." [6] It is "lyrical philosophy and possibly the first conscious attempt to express an individual philosophy lyrically. . . ." [7] Thus, in *Wood Note*, he concludes a brief sketch with lines which suggest a mysterious spiritual presence in the woods and the unreality of matter:

Of what vast deep is this the echo?
Of what old dreams the answer? *(Moods,* p. 17)

God, for the poet of *Moods*, is present in all things and in the humblest of men:

God
To my astonishment
Is shining my shoes.
He has taken the form,
In part,
Of an Italian shoe black
Who is eager to earn a dime . . .
Reading a newspaper
To learn of Himself
I presume . . .
Getting drunk,
Eating a ham sandwich
In order to maintain His strength.
A most varied
Restless
Changeful
Moody
God. . . . (pp. 91-92) [8]

In his lyrical moods, Dreiser mystically identifies himself with this changeful God and, like Proteus, in the poem which bears this name, becomes, in turn:

Birds flying in the air over a river,
And children playing in a meadow beside it,
A stream that turns an ancient wheel
Under great trees,
And cattle in the water
Below the trees,
And sun, and shade,
And warmth, and grass,
And myself
And not myself
Dreaming in the grass. . . . (p. 7)

But, strangely enough, this keen perception of an underlying mystery in all things is again and again spoiled so to speak, by a disquieting sense of the purposelessness and meaninglessness of the

world, in *The Passing Freight,* for instance, in which the disillusioned poet dejectedly meditates on the passage of a train:

> Out of the mystery
> And meaninglessness of things
> And into it again;
> A train bearing cotton
> With thunder and smoke
> And a flare of fire,
> Yet bearing that
> Which is nothing more than an idea;
> That has come out of the darkness of chemistry
> And will soon return into it . . .
>
> And I, myself,
> Who view it
> And admire—
> Out of the mystery
> And meaninglessness of things
> And into them again. (pp. 54-55)

In the same way, in *Ephemeron,* instead of buoyantly singing his self
like Whitman he bitterly complains, like Clyde Griffiths, of being
"betrayed,"

> But not by the thousand impossible Gods
> Of mine [i.e., man's] own invention
> To whom I have yearningly
> And hopelessly prayed,
> But by mine own lacks
> And insufficiencies
> That are not of my creating.
> Ask me not whose. (p. 58)

And he resignedly concludes in a fit of depression:

> Too tired—
> And indifferent

To be a part of that
That has no meaning—
Is not that the ultimate
And is not that
A justification
And
The greater wisdom? (p. 311)

At such times we seem to be a very long way indeed from Emerson's boundless optimism. Dreiser's position is then almost that of an agnostic. We are reminded of the sceptical utterances with which he had sprinkled *A Traveler at Forty:*

> For myself, I accept now no creeds. I do not know what truth is, what beauty is, what love is, what hope is. I do not believe any one absolutely and I do not doubt any one absolutely. . . . I indict nature here and now . . . as being aimless, pointless, unfair, unjust. I see in the whole thing no scheme, but an accidental one—no justice save accidental justice. (pp. 4, 42)

But such statements expressed only "moods," to take up his own word. They corresponded to only one facet of his thought. Emerson too did not always yield himself to "the perfect whole," [9] and had to admit that "our torment is Unbelief, the Uncertainty as to what we ought to do; the distrust of the value of what we do, and the distrust that the Necessity (which we all at last believe in) is fair and beneficent," [10] But, like Emerson, Dreiser succeeded in transcending his doubts—even though he never entirely discarded them—and in some of his *Moods* he prays "the hidden God," "the substance of suns, and flowers, rats and kings" (p. 197), and worships with the fervor of a true transcendentalist:

Yet I must pray,—
Pray.
And do.
I lift up my hands.
I kneel.

I seek in heart
Because I must,—
Must. (p. 178)

Honor that spirit in man
That, in the face of shame
And failure,
Still dreams of better things.

Give honor unto him
Who, in the midst of doubt . . .
Still, still can dream
And still build temples—
Not to Christ,
Or Buddha,
But to Beauty—
The human will to loveliness. (p. 154)

Beauty,
Its worship,
Shall never die. (p. 327)

Like the transcendentalists, what Dreiser means by beauty is not plastic beauty, but the mysterious presence behind appearances of something wonderful which escapes his senses. His apprehension of beauty is in fact a mystical intuition, a form of religious worship:

Behind this seeming substance
Of reality . . .
Picturing something
Seeking something
The image of our dreams. (p. 306)

What he keeps seeking and wondering at is the enigmatic force which carries all things forward irresistibly toward an unknown destination. He ultimately equates reality with Life. In *Protoplast*, he represents the world as

A substance that is not flesh
Or thought
Or reality
But the likeness,
The wish,
The dream, mayhap,
Of something that is eternal,
But will not rest
Or stay
In any form. (p. 249)

He worships life in all its forms—life "as it is," to take the words
which he himself used to define his realism (and this incidentally
shows that there was after all no fundamental incompatibility between his transcendentalism and his naturalism). He felt a "Creative Force" at work in the world, "the amazing Creative force
which has brought 'humanity' along with its entire environment
into being." [11] According to him, "man is not really and truly
living and thinking, but, on the contrary, is being lived and
thought by that which has produced him. Apart from it . . . he has
no existence." [12] In 1940, writing to Miss Dorothy Payne Davis,
who had maintained in a Master's thesis submitted to Loyola University of the South that he believed "in God and the immortality
of the soul even though [he called] it the unintelligible," he affirmed:

All things to me are emanations and evolutions of cosmic
forces and cosmic laws. Buddha and Mary Baker Eddy af-
firmed an *over* or *one* universal soul, itself *being* and so *containing*
all wisdom and all creative power. Modern science sees no
other answer than this, but it is not willing to affirm it . . . As
for the human soul—my scientific as well as my philosophic
studies compel me to feel that there can be but one primary
creative force or soul, the discoverable physical as well as
chemical laws of which appear to be obeyed by all matter and
energy—or matter-energy. I think of all creatures or "creations" as material or energy constructions and so mani-

festations of whatsoever force it is that occupies space and
expresses itself as matter or energy—or matter-energy. *(Letters . . , vol. III, pp. 886-89.)*

Emerson's "oversoul" thus becomes identified with energy as conceived by modern physicists:

> Energy,
> Color,
> Form,
> Tone,
> Mingle and make "Life." (p. 127)

Therefore, in Whitman's own words, "the smallest sprout shows
there is really no death" *(Song of Myself,* sec. 6, l. 28):

> My span is brief
> But my world-flower,—
> It blooms
> Forever. (p. 170)

"There is in my judgment no death," he declared more explicitly
in *A Traveler at Forty,* "the universe is composed of life; but nevertheless, I cannot see any continuous life for any individual" (p.
448).

As with transcendentalists, this dynamic vitalism leads up to a
wish to live rather than expiate,[13] to self-reliance and the exaltation of individualism. Dreiser did not believe in original sin or the
innate corruption of man any more than Emerson. All his characters are men of good will. True, they are eminently fallible, but
they are not really responsible for their lapses since they are caught
in a tangle of biological and social forces which, to a large extent,
determine their behavior. For Dreiser there is no such thing as
"sin":

> Come now—
> The thing which you call sin

Is still not sin to me,
Or you. (pp. 18-19)

And he curses conscience, that troublesome interrupter, that "whispering, pushing thing," that "damned equation / Between the weak and strong, The wise and foolish" (ibid.). On the contrary, he glorifies instincts and the desire for pleasure and, above all, exalts the "divine afflatus" of love which "gives color, force and beauty" to those who are lightened by its touch.[14] He celebrates what he calls "the rich upwelling force of life and love." [15] Like Whitman, he likes "big, raw, crude, hungry men who are eager for gain—for self-glorification." [16] He hoped for more "great individuals among women as well as among men." [17] Like Emerson, he believed in "representative men":

> The world is always struggling to express itself. . . . Most people are not capable of voicing their feelings. They depend upon others. That is what genius is for. One man expresses their desire for them in music; another one in poetry; another one in a play. . . . As harps in the wind [they voice] in their moods all the ebb and flow of the ideal. *(Sister Carrie,* pp. 537, 555).

His Cowperwood is such a man—"a kind of superman . . . impelled by some blazing internal force which hurried him on and on," a "significant individual" doing "what his instincts tell him to do," "rushing like a great comet to the zenith" and illuminating "the terrors and wonders of individuality." [18] *The Financier* and *The Titan* constitute an apotheosis of individualism. Dreiser himself once declared in an interview that he was too "intense an individualist" to believe in socialism.[19] As a matter of fact, he was such a self-reliant individualist that he proudly entitled one of his travel-books *Dreiser Looks at Russia,* as if he had been Emerson's "transparent eyeball" at the center of the universe.

All these resemblances between transcendentalism and Dreiser's philosophy were not accidental. In his youth, Dreiser read Emerson's works with passion. In 1940, when Edgar Lee Masters sent

him a copy of his Emerson book, *The Living Thoughts of Emerson,*
Dreiser wrote to him enthusiastically:

> . . . it's been so long that I looked into Emerson that I sat
> down and read the most of it and found it fascinating. As a
> matter of fact I find these condensations . . . have the value of
> fresh creative writing—an entirely new work. For so much that
> is prolix and not absolutely essential is done away with and
> you have the sense of something brisk, highly integrated and
> of tremendous as well as delightful import. At least this is true
> of your Emerson volume. *(Letters . . . ,* vol. III, pp. 873-74)

In another letter of the same period he quoted a stanza of "Emerson's interpretive [*sic*] *Brahma"* (ibid., p. 887), for he was as vitally
interested as Emerson in oriental mysticism. In *The Titan,* he even
made Berenice Fleming, the heroine, study with a Guru in India
for four years and sound the philosophical abysses of Brahmanism.
He was also an admirer of Thoreau. He had compiled a book
entitled *Thoreau's Living Thoughts* for the same series in which Edgar
Lee Masters's condensation of Emerson appeared, and he wrote of
it: "I felt . . . that I had gotten together a body of real thought most
valuable to me if no other" (ibid., p. 874). He was even acquainted
with the teachings of Elias Hicks, the Quaker heretic, whom Whitman had heard preach when a child and respected so much.[20]
Dreiser declared that Elias Hicks's creed constituted "the most
reasonable of religions." [21]

So transcendentalism undeniably exerted an influence on his
thought. But its importance should not be exaggerated. There was
a sort of preestablished harmony between the transcendentalists
and himself. Their writings merely encouraged him to preserve
and develop, instead of suppressing or repressing, the mystical
tendencies of his temperament. Even as a child he was an exceptionally sensitive lover of nature endowed with a keen sense of
wonder which he never lost. In *Dawn* he describes himself as a

> child of three or four and standing at a gate looking up a road
> and wondering if the sky actually came down to the street as it
> seemed to . . . or . . . sitting of an evening watching the trees,

the sky, the setting sun, and feeling an intense emotional stir of beauty, so wonderful, so strange, so new, that I recall it even now, he added, as if it had been a moving and appealing strain of music.[22]

He also notes in the same book that, when a little older, though he soon realized "the futility of prayer," he nevertheless staunchly believed that "there must be a land somewhere to which I belonged and where I could fly" (p. 60).

This innate sense of the mystery and beauty of the world, which his transcendentalism no doubt reinforced, illuminates not only his poems, but also his so-called naturalistic novels. It glows even in *An American Tragedy,* which is probably the most prosaic of his books. Instead of describing "Life as it is," he often looks at it through the wondering eyes of Clyde Griffiths, who stares at the rich and their dwellings and feels "like looking through the gates of Paradise" (p. 57). Reality often gives place to dreams, dreams of beauty and wealth and pleasure. The novel was at first to be entitled *Mirages,*[23] an unexpected title for a naturalistic study, but a fitting one for this strange story in which the material world at times becomes something unsubstantial:

> To be sure, there was Roberta over there, but by now she had faded to a shadow or thought really, a form of illusion more vaporous than real . . . she was very insubstantial . . . (p. 528)

Dreiser's sense of wonder is so intense that it occasionally enables him to clothe with beauty the most commonplace and even the most vulgar sights:

> . . . there would gather on her upper lip and chin and forehead little beads of perspiration which . . . like jewels . . . only seemed to enhance her charm. (p. 278)

Moreover, Dreiser constantly suggests intangible things (there are at least three cases of telepathy in *An American Tragedy*) and, generally speaking, we feel him haunted by the mystery of the universe, the wonder of life, and the terror of death, by what he calls "the beauty of the days—of the sun and rain—of work, love, energy, desire" (p. 864).

As to the characters—at least the major ones—they are essentially forces which move forward and come into conflict with other forces, but they have no idiosyncrasies, no minor traits. They are never sharply individualized. They remind the reader of Mayakowsky's "clouds in trousers," for their clothes are carefully described, but, though they have bodies full of appetites and desires, they have no faces. Dreiser's point of view is not psychological, but social *and* metaphysical. He is not interested in his characters as individuals, but as social types *and* as manifestations of the central life force which flows through all things, as parts of the "oversoul."

Besides, most of these characters constantly aspire to something beyond the workaday world in which they are caught. They crave a fuller life, beauty, some ideal which they are unable to define, but in whose existence they firmly believe. In *Sister Carrie* in particular, Dreiser again and again suggests "that constant drag to something better" which Carrie feels so strongly (p. 114), but it is not particular to her, it is a universal feeling, according to Dreiser. He makes her face "representative of all desire" and warns us that "her look was something which represented the world's longing" (p. 337). She is a transcendentalist poet in her own silent way when she rocks in her chair and dreams:

> Sitting alone, she was now an illustration of the devious ways by which one who feels, rather than reasons, may be led in the pursuit of beauty. . . . Oh, Carrie, Carrie! Oh, blind strivings of the human heart! Onward, onward, it saith, and where beauty leads, there it follows. (p. 557)

In short, to use his own words, she yields to "the lure of the spirit." [24]

Dreiser's transcendentalism also accounts for the images which at times unexpectedly bloom in the drabbest realistic passages. They are never very remarkable, or original, but they are meant to suggest the wonder of life and the craving of the characters for some unattainable and undefinable ideal. In the same way, the chapter headings in *Sister Carrie* transmute the prosaic contents of the various chapters into something rich and strange—though they are for the most part borrowed from such operas as "Sinbad the Sailor" and "Ali Baba and the Forty Thieves," which Dreiser saw in Chicago. They metamorphose everyday reality into something mysterious and suggest the existence of another world beyond mere appearances.

Dreiser, thus, instead of minutely and objectively describing the more or less sordid background of his characters, again and again allows himself to be carried away by his imagination—and his imagination is not mere fancy, but that poetic faculty which Coleridge in his *Biographia Literaria* defined as "an esemplastic power." It adds "the gleam, / The light that never was, on sea or land, The consecration, and the Poet's dream," as Wordsworth said.[25] And Dreiser was perfectly aware of it. He even used the same words as Wordsworth, not only in one of his *Moods*, where he referred to

> The high suggestion of a world that never was
> On earth or sea (p. 296)

but also in *Dawn*, where he warns us that "The City of which [he is] now about to write [namely Chicago] never was on land or sea," for even "if it appears to have the outlines of reality, he adds, they are but shadow to the glory that was in [his] own mind" (p. 156).

Thanks to the intervention of this quasi-mystical faculty, when we read Dreiser's novels, we are again and again reminded of the cosmic context of his characters' lives. His books are not mere naturalistic studies of social conditions; we are never allowed to forget the presence of an infinite and mysterious universe in the background. Carrie, for instance, is made to look "at the blue sky overhead with more realisation of its charm than had ever come to her before" (p. 20). She sits "looking out upon the night and streets in silent wonder" (p. 15). To her, as

> to a child . . . the approach to a great city for the first time is a wonderful thing. Particularly if it be evening—that mystic pe-

riod between the glare and gloom of the world when life is changing from one sphere or condition to another. Ah, the promise of the night. (p. 9)

And, on another occasion, "she tripped along, the clear sky pouring liquid blue into her soul. Oh, blessed are the children of endeavor in this, that they try and are hopeful," Dreiser adds, "and blessed also are they who, knowing, smile and approve" (p. 188). There is no trace of a Marxist interpretation of American society in all this. In such passages, Dreiser merely wants to convey his sense of the totality and oneness of the world. This form of cosmic imagination must have been inborn in him, but he may also have deliberately cultivated it. For, in *An American Tragedy*, the Reverend MacMillan prescribes the following spiritual exercise to Clyde Griffiths:

> You have a Bible. . . . Open to St. John. Read it all—over and over. Think and pray—and think on all the things about you—the moon, the stars, the sun, the trees, the sea—your own beating heart, your body and strength. . . . (p. 840)

Now this recommendation strangely resembles the following note which has been found among Whitman's papers:

> First of all prepare for study by the following self-teaching exercises. Abstract yourself from this book; realize where you are at present located, the point you stand that is now to you the centre of all. Look up overhead, think of space stretching out, think of all the unnumbered orbs wheeling safely there, invisible to us by day, some visible by night. . . . Spend some minutes faithfully in this exercise. . . .[26]

So it seems that, in order to reach a state of grace, Dreiser practiced the same kind of spiritual exercises as the poet who sang himself and the cosmos.

Thus, Dreiser was a poet and in several respects a belated transcendentalist in his naturalistic novels as well as in his poems.

True, his transcendentalism coexisted with lurking doubts that prevented him from giving any dogmatic content to his intuitions and with a tenacious pessimism that made it impossible for him to ignore social and other evils, but, nevertheless, he spontaneously sensed beneath this world of appearances another inward world which he kept wondering at and whose universal presence conferred beauty and mystery on the most banal and insignificant sights. Without this poetical power his works would be nothing but dull naturalistic descriptions of American society, whereas, thanks to it, he has, however massively, sung himself and celebrated—or pitied—himself in the guise of various characters ("Sister Carrie, Cowperwood, Clyde Griffiths, c'est moi," he might have exclaimed), and, at the same time, he sang and celebrated man and the presence in man of the irresistible creative force at work in the world. His transcendentalism is therefore the true source of his greatness.

Notes

1. Cf. Alfred Kazin's chapter on Dreiser in *On Native Grounds* and his introduction to *The Stature of Theodore Dreiser,* ed. by A. Kazin and Charles Shapiro (Bloomington: Indiana University Press, 1955). The latter book contains a fine essay by Charles Child Walcutt on "Theodore Dreiser and the Divided Stream" (pp. 246-69). Cf. also the chapter on "Dreiser's Philosophy" in F. O. Matthiessen's *Dreiser* (New York, 1951).
2. Cf. Emerson's statement in *Self-Reliance:* "Suppose you should contradict yourself; what then?" which Whitman echoed in the famous lines: "Do I contradict myself? / Very well then, I contradict myself . . . ." "Song of Myself," sec. 51.
3. *A Traveler at Forty* (New York, 1914), p. 34.
4. The first edition, to which we will refer henceforward, was limited to 550 copies and published in New York in 1926. A second edition, enlarged and illustrated, came out in 1928, and a third one, further revised and enlarged, in 1935.
5. Cf. a letter to H. L. Mencken dated March 8, 1943, in *Letters of Theodore Dreiser, A Selection,* ed. by Robert H. Elias (University of Pennsylvania Press, 1959), vol. III, p. 979.
6. Letter to Richard L. Simon, Feb. 5, 1935, ibid., vol. II, p. 722.
7. Letter to Miss Ish-Kishor, Feb. 14, 1935, ibid., p. 728.
8. This poem is entitled *All in All,* a title which recalls Emerson's *Each in All.*

9. Cf. last line of *Each in All.*
10. Essay on *The Times.*
11. In a letter to Mencken quoted by Elias, *Theodore Dreiser, Apostle of Nature* (New York, 1949), p. 279.
12. *The Myth of Individuality in American Mercury,* vol. XXXI (1934), p. 341.
13. "I do not wish to expiate but to live." Emerson, *Self-Reliance.*
14. *Sister Carrie,* Modern Library Ed., p. 179.
15. *An American Tragedy,* Modern Library Ed., p.327.
16. *A Traveler at Forty,* p. 778.
17. Quoted by Elias in *Theodore Dreiser,* p. 169.
18. Quoted by C. C. Walcutt in *The Stature of Theodore Dreiser,* p. 259.
19. *New York Evening Post,* Jan. 11. 1927.
20. Cf. his essay on Elias Hicks in *Specimen Days.*
21. *Boston Evening Transcript,* Jan. 29, 1927.
22. *Dawn* (New York, 1931), pp. 16-17.
23. A passage in Book I, Chap. IV (p. 38), still recalls this early title: "Decidedly this simple and yet idyllic compound of the commonplace had all the luster and wonder of a spiritual transfiguration, the true image of the lost and thirsting and seeking victim of the desert."
24. Title of chapter 20. Initially Dreiser thought of entitling the book *The Flesh and the Spirit,* a true transcendentalist title.
25. *Peele Castle,* ll. 14-16.
26. Quoted in my essay on "Whitman's Fundamental Aesthetics" in *Walt Whitman Abroad,* ed. by Gay W. Allen (Syracuse University Press, 1955), p. 97.

8.

Eugene O'Neill's Transcendental Phase

Though to all appearances O'Neill was primarily a playwright and an experimenter with dramatic forms who never considered himself a thinker, he was in fact desperately trying to express "something" in all his plays. He chose drama as a medium, but, for all his interest in technique, he never considered it an end in itself, but rather a means to live by proxy a certain number of problems which obsessed him. In *Lazarus Laughed,* he speaks of men as "those haunted heroes." Actually this is less a definition of mankind than a description of himself. He composed plays because he had to write in order to liberate himself and exorcise ghosts. It was a compulsion. The result was plays because of his environment, because his father was an actor and he was an "enfant de la balle," but it might have been novels just as well, and he would probably have written better novels than plays, for he was constantly hampered by the limitations of the stage. In his case literary creation was not a gratuitous activity, but an intense imaginative experience, an *Erlebnis.* He lived it. It was a passionate answer to the problems which tormented him with excruciating strength. This is no mere figure of speech. He roamed the world for years in search of a solution, trying to find a remedy for his fundamental despair, giving up the comfort and security of family life and nearly losing his health and life in the process.

After his wandering years, his *Wanderjahre,* when his health broke down and he was obliged to bring his restless comings-and-goings to a close, he went on exploring the world in imagination, not as a dilettante or a tourist in the realms of thought, but as a passionate pilgrim in quest of a shrine at which to worship. Though brought up a Roman Catholic, he lost his faith as an adolescent. Yet his nature abhorred this spiritual vacuum and he ardently looked for a substitute ever after. His religious faith was killed by rationalism and scientific materialism, but the restlessness and violence of his quest for a personal religion sprang from no coldly rational intellect.

Each of his plays is thus not only an experiment in craftsmanship, but also an attempt to find God or at least some justification for the flagrant inconsistencies of the human condition. His interest was less in psychology than in metaphysics. He said so himself in a letter to Joseph Wood Krutch: "Most modern plays are concerned with the relation between man and man, but that does not interest me at all. I am interested only in the relation between man and God." [1]

In spite of its apparent dramatic directness, therefore, *Desire under the Elms* is essentially, like his other plays, a philosophical tragedy about man and God rather than a naturalistic chunk of life depicting the mores of a bunch of clumsy New England rustics.

Reduced to essentials in this very primitive setting, man appears primarily as an animal. The first specimens whom we have a chance to observe when the curtain rises, Eben and especially Simeon and Peter, look like oxen, eat, work, and behave like a team of oxen, and feel tied up to the other animals of the farm by bonds of brotherhood: ". . . the cows knows us. . . . An' the hosses, an' pigs, an' chickens. . . . They knows us like brothers—and likes us" (Part I, scene 4).[2] They obey their instincts blindly and think only of drinking, eating, and fornicating. Their lust is quite literally bestial, as shown by Eben's account of his visit to Min: "I begun t'beller like a calf an' cuss at the same time . . . an' she got scared, an' I just grabbed holt an' tuk her" (Part I, scene 3).[3] When Abbie courts

Eben, the scene is not much different. She kisses him greedily and at first he submits dumbly, but soon, after returning her kisses, he hurls her away from him and, O'Neill tells us, "they stand speechless and breathless, panting like two animals" (Part II, scene 2).[4]

These inarticulate, animal-like creatures differ from their dumb brothers in only one respect (but it is hardly an improvement): they are possessed with the mania for owning things, whether gold or land. They all crave money or title deeds. In short, they bear a strong family likeness to Swift's Yahoos. They have only one redeeming feature: an embryonic sense of beauty which makes them exclaim "purty" in a rather monotonous manner whenever they notice the beauty of their surroundings. The only exception is the sheriff, who at the very end of the play passes very matter-of-fact and anticlimactic comments on the salable value of the farm while Eben and Abbie admire the beauty of the sunrise.

Far from being a free agent, man is thus by and large the slave of his instincts, and O'Neill here revives the old Calvinistic dogma of predestination. As early as his very first play, *The Web*, of the transparent title, he attempted to show that man is caught in a web of circumstances, a web that is not of his own weaving. At the end of *The Web*, O'Neill tells us that Rose, the prostitute, "seems to be aware of something in the room which none of the others can see—perhaps the personification of the ironic life force that has crushed her."[5] In *Desire under the Elms*, Eben feels trapped in exactly the same way: "Each day," the stage directions inform us, "is a cage in which he finds himself trapped."[6] He is indeed trapped by circumstances—tied up to that bleak New England farm which he somehow considers part of his mother, and he is also psychologically trapped by an all-powerful mother complex which unknown to him determines his whole behavior toward his father as well as toward women in general. His temperament is wholly determined by his heredity: it is a combination of his mother's softness and lack of will, as his father again and again points out, and of his father's aggressiveness and obstinacy, as his two elder brothers repeatedly tell us: "he is a chip of the old block, the spitting image of his father. . . ."

As for Abbie, she is just as trapped as he is. When she enters the stage, we are warned that she has "the same unsettled, untamed, desperate quality which is so apparent in Eben." [7] And shortly afterward we learn that she "was a orphan early an' had t'wuk fur others in other folks' hums," and her first husband "turned out a drunken spreer" and got sick and died. She then felt free again only to discover that all she was free for was to work again "in other folks' hums, doin' other folks' wuk" till she had almost given up hope of ever doing her own work in her own home (Part I, scene 4).[8]

Ephraim Cabot himself, for all his will power and vigor, is caught in the same web as the others. His whole behavior is conditioned by his Puritan upbringing. He cannot think of anything but work, hard work on a barren New England farm. *Laborare est orare,* Carlyle claimed, "work is worship." Ephraim Cabot is a degenerate Puritan. Work has ceased to be a form of worship for him, yet he believes in its virtue and absolute value because he has been brought up that way. He once tried to escape his self-imposed serfdom. Like many other New Englanders, he went West and in the broad meadows of the central plains found black soil as rich as gold, without a stone. He had only to plough and sow and then sit and smoke his pipe and watch things grow. He could have become a rich man and led an easy and idle life, but he preferred to give it up and return to his New England farm and to hard work on a stony soil,[9] which proves the extraordinary strength of his Puritan compulsions. They practically deprived him of his freedom of choice.

So, at the start at least, the three major characters of *Desire under the Elms* are not free. They bear psychological or moral chains. Consequently, they cannot be held responsible for their actions, and Simeon with his pleasant shrewdness is perfectly aware of it. When Eben accuses his father of killing his "Maw," Simeon retorts: "No one never kills nobody. It's allus somethin' that's the murderer" (Part I, scene 2).[10] "Somethin'," that is to say one of those mysterious things which impel men to act this way or that, whether they like it or not, whether they are aware of it or not. This is a modified form of Puritan pessimism: all men are sinners in the clutches of Satan—or of God who is always "nagging his sheep to sin" (Part I, scene 4),[11] the better to punish them afterward, always ready to smite His undutiful sons with His worst curse.

How can a man save his soul under such circumstances? Though, theoretically, O'Neill's approach is strictly nontheological and he is not concerned with the problem of salvation, he is constantly obsessed with it all the same, and in this play, he gives it a Nietzschean answer: passion. Passion alone, he suggests, can enable man to transcend his animal nature. He repeatedly exalts the purity and transfiguring power of love. Eben's passion for Abbie, which at first is mere lust, soon becomes love—and there is a difference in kind between the two. The passage from lust to love is similar to the transmutation of lead into gold. Whereas lust, which is tied to the body, is finite and transient, love, which transcends the body, is infinite and eternal. Abbie kills her infant son to prove her love to Eben, and at the end of scene 3 of Part III proclaims that her love for Eben will never change, whatever he does to her. The play ends on an apotheosis of love. The two lovers stand "looking up raptly in attitudes strangely aloof and devout" at the "purty" rising sun, which contrasts with the pallid setting sun that lit up the opening of the play, at a time when everything took place on the plane of coarse material things and lust.

Man can thus be redeemed by a great passion and save his soul and attain grandeur. The farm under the elms, which looked so sordid when the curtain rose, witnesses a sublime *dénouement* and at the end almost becomes one of those places where the spirit bloweth.

The reason for this extraordinary change is that, in Hamlet's words:

There are more things in heaven and earth . . .
Than are dreamt of in all [our] philosophy,

as Cabot again feels, for all his hardness and insensitivity: "They's thin's pokin' about in the dark—in the corners" (Part II, scene 2).[12] "Even the music can't drive it out—somethin'. Ye kin feel it droppin' off the elums, climbin' up the roof, sneakin' down the chimney, pokin' in the corners. They's no peace in houses, they's no rest livin' with folks. Somethin's always livin' with ye" . . . (Part III, scene 2).[13]

What is that "somethin' " whose presence disturbs him? It is the "Desire" of the title—an irresistible life-force (somewhat similar to G. B. Shaw's), which flows through the elms and through old Cabot himself sometimes, as when it makes him leave his farm in spring and go in search of a new wife. But it is especially powerful in Eben and Abbie. It is that thing which makes Eben look like a wild animal in captivity when he enters the stage, and feel "inwardly unsubdued." It is quite impersonal, and Eben refers to it in the neuter: "I kin feel it growin' in me—growin' an' growin'—till it'll bust out" (Part I, scene 2).[14] It is the magnetic force which draws Eben to Abbie through walls and partitions (Part II, scene 2). It is Nature—and Abbie intones a hymn to her—or it—in her own inarticulate way when she presses Eben to yield to his passion: "Hain't the sun strong an' hot? Ye kin feel it burnin' into the earth—Nature—makin' thin's grow—bigger 'n' bigger—burnin' inside ye—makin' ye want t'grow—into somethin' else—till ye are jined with it—an' it's your 'n—but it owns ye—too—an' makes ye grow bigger—like a tree—like them elums" (Part II, scene 1).[15]

In short, the "Desire" which flows through the elms and drips from them and pervades everything under them is God—though the word is never used. It is not, however, the God of the Christians, but rather a dynamic, impersonal, pantheistic, or panpsychistic deity present in all things, whether animate or inanimate, breaking barriers between individuals as in the case of Eben and Abbie, dissolving their lonesomeness and making them feel one. In a way it is a pagan God, a Dionysian deity, for it partly manifests itself in the form of carnal desire. Under its influence, Eben and Cabot become inspired poets (in prose) and sing woman, the lovely incarnation of the soft and warm goddess of fertility and life: "She's like t'night, she's soft 'n' warm, her eyes kin wink like a star, her mouth's wa'm, her arms 're wa'm, she smells like a wa'm plowed field, she's purty" (Part I, scene 2).[16] "Yew air my Rose o' Sharon! Behold! yew air fair; yer eyes air doves; yer lips air like scarlet; yer two breasts air like two fawns; yer navel be like a round goblet; yer belly be like a heap o' wheat,' exclaims old Cabot, echoing chapters 4 and 7 of the Song of Solomon.[17]

The omnipresent God is fundamentally a cosmic sexual urge, spontaneous, beautiful, unselfish, and amoral. In this perspective the notion of sin becomes meaningless. "He was the child of our sin," says Eben of the baby, but Abbie proudly answers "as if defying God" (the God of the Christians): "I don't repent that sin. I ain't askin' God t'fergive that" (Part III, scene 4).[18] The two lovers have gone back to the Garden of Eden from which Adam and Eve were expelled. They have become "Children of Adam," to take up Walt Whitman's phrase.

The life-force, the desire which circulates through the elms as well as through the *dramatis personae,* is the very reverse of the God worshipped by Ephraim Cabot, which has the hardness and immobility of a stone—and the sterility of one (Part II, scene 2). His God is the God of repression and lonesomeness and hard work—the God humorously called up by Robert Frost in "Of the Stones of the Place," and to some extent a duplicate of Robinson Jeffers's anti-human God.

Abbie, on the contrary, recommends yielding to the life impulse, letting Nature speak at every hazard "without check with original energy." [19] It is against nature, it is impious, she claims, to resist its will: "It's agin nature, Eben. Ye been fightin' yer nature ever since the day I come" . . . (Part II, scene 1).[20] With her, Emerson's Nature has acquired sex.

This is a combination of Nietzsche's Dionysian philosophy and Freudianism, and in *Desire under the Elms* it leads— in spite of the Dostoevskian quality of the *Crime and Punishment* situation at the end of the play—to an optimistic conclusion: the couple Eben-Abbie is not crushed by adverse circumstances. They have fulfilled themselves, they have fully lived and, far from being driven to despair by their trials, they are full of a strange "hopeless hope" when the curtain falls.

In this play we thus witness the dramatic clash of two opposite philosophies: Old Cabot's Puritanism and Abbie's worship of Dionysius—a conflict between the stones of the former and the elms of the latter, which O'Neill himself seems to have experienced throughout his life. He obviously sympathized with warm uninhibited characters like Eben and Abbie in *Desire under the Elms* and with Marie Brantome and Christine in *Mourning Becomes Electra,* though he never was warm and uninhibited himself. In everyday life, except when he was under the influence of alcohol, he was to some extent closer to Cabot than to Eben. Other things being equal, he suffered from the same dichotomy as Dr. Jekyll. Two men were at war within him. He was both Billy Brown and Dion Anthony. But the twain never fused. He was probably thinking of his own predicament when he made Dion, "life's lover," complain in *The Great God Brown* "with a suffering bewilderment": "Why am I afraid to dance, I who love music and rhythm and grace and song and laughter? Why am I afraid to live, I who love life and the beauty of flesh and the living colors of the earth and sky and sea? Why am I afraid of love, I who love love? . . . Why must I be so ashamed of my strength, so proud of my weakness"? (Prologue).[21] He would have liked freely to worship "the Great God Pan," [22] as Dion calls him; instead of that he had to bear "the intolerable cilice of life." [23] He would have liked to laugh with Lazarus and shout like Lazarus's followers:

> There is only life
> There is only laughter (Act II, scene 1),[24]

but his ingrained masochistic catholicism made laughter die on his lips. *Desire under the Elms* is the secret expression of his poignant nostalgia for a joy of life he was unable to experience.

However, his personal failure and his acute awareness of the cruelty of the human condition did not prevent him from concluding that life is a vivid and exciting experience well worth the trouble to the very end. And that is why Abbie and Eben do not commit suicide in the last act, and even Lavinia refuses to kill herself in *Mourning Becomes Electra,* thus breaking one of the most imperative laws of tragedy. O'Neill's ultimate attitude to life during this nostalgic period (1923 to 1926) is best expressed by the hero of *The Great God Brown:* "I've loved, lusted, won and lost, sung and wept" (Act II, scene 2).[25] And anyway, as O'Neill proclaimed in *Lazarus Laughed* in conformity with Nietzsche's teachings: "Men are . . . unimportant . . . Man remains . . . For Man death is not." The same life-force flows through all men, and whatever their personal limitations may be, whether they are bums, drunken sailors, or New England farmers, it endows them all with tragic grandeur. All individuals are potentially as worthy of interest as the mighty kings and queens of Greek tragedies. *Desire under the Elms* is thus the quiet affirmation of the fundamental dignity of all men in a godless (?) universe—or at least in a universe deprived of the help and support of the personal God posited by Christianity.

Notes

1. Quoted by Joseph Wood Krutch in his introduction to the Modern Library Edition of O'Neill's *Nine Plays*, p. xvii.
2. Ibid., p. 152.
3. Ibid., p. 148.
4. Ibid., p. 174.
5. *Ten Lost Plays* (New York: Random House, 1964), p. 53.
6. *Nine Plays*, p. 137.
7. Ibid., p. 155.
8. Ibid., p. 160.
9. Ibid., p. 172.
10. Ibid., p. 141.
11. Ibid., p. 161.
12. Ibid., p. 174.
13. Ibid., p. 189.
14. Ibid., p. 144.
15. Ibid., p. 164.
16. Ibid., p. 145.
17. Ibid., p. 167.
18. Ibid., p. 203.
19. Walt Whitman, "Song of Myself," *Leaves of Grass*, sec. 1, ll. 1, 13.
20. *Nine Plays*, p. 164.
21. Ibid., p. 315.
22. Ibid., p. 318.
23. Ibid., p. 375.
24. Ibid., p. 418.
25. Ibid., p. 347.

9.

Sherwood Anderson's
Transcendentalist Aesthetics

When *Winesburg, Ohio,* appeared in 1919, people saw nothing but its realism or naturalism. It was hailed as a masterpiece of naturalism by reviewers who read it through Dreiser. Francis Hackett, for instance, called Sherwood Anderson "a naturalist with a skirl of music." [1] It seemed to him and other critics that Anderson's main concern was an attempt to copy reality as faithfully and accurately as possible without shrinking from the coarser aspects of life. There is some truth in this, but it is not the whole truth, for, even if Sherwood Anderson in 1917 wrote an essay entitled "An Apology for Crudity" and did believe in the necessity of describing crude things, *Winesburg, Ohio,* is not at all an attempt to reproduce the seamy side of life slavishly and without selection, and it does not record external appearances only.

At first sight, however, the stories which make up *Winesburg, Ohio,* offer a satisfactory cross-section of village life in the Middle West in the author's time. Both the background and the characters are authentic. It has been proved that Sherwood Anderson used childhood memories, and Winesburg is the Clyde of his boyhood with hardly any change.[2] He even preserved some of the original

124

names of streets and tradespeople. There are indeed passages which read like descriptions in a guidebook:

> Cowley & Son's store did not face the main street of Winesburg. The front was on Maumee Street and beyond it was Voight's wagon shop and a shed for the sheltering of farmers' horses. Beside the store an alleyway ran behind the main street stores and all day drays and delivery wagons, intent on bringing in and taking out goods, passed up and down. The store itself was indescribable. . . . In the window facing Maumee Street stood a chunk of coal as large as an apple barrel, to indicate that orders for coal were taken, and beside the black mass of the coal stood three combs of honey grown brown and dirty in their wooden frames.[3]

At times we have the impression of thumbing a collection of old picture postcards. The topographic and photographic realism is impeccable, and the observer remains as cold and detached as the lens of a camera. He shows no emotion and never smiles. He does not idealize, either, by smoothing over unpleasant details. As Sherwood Anderson himself said in *Tar:* "Being a realist in his writing and thinking, Tar [that is to say, himself] did not make the houses of his town very comfortable or the people particularly good or in any way exceptional." [4]

The characters and their experiences are depicted in the same spirit of objectivity and complete neutrality:

> One afternoon a man of the town, Henry Bradford, who kept a saloon, came to the schoolhouse door. Calling Adolph Myers into the school yard he began to beat him with his fists. As his hard knuckles beat down into the frightened face of the school master, his wrath became more and more terrible. Screaming with dismay, the children ran here and there like disturbed insects. . . .[5]

In such passages, Sherwood Anderson purposely confines himself to describing the behavior of the actors. True, it is not behaviorism properly speaking, since, to some extent, he interprets the gestures and screams which he describes and uses such words as "frightened" and "dismay" to help us understand what is taking place in the minds of the characters, but he passes no judgments and in appearance does not take sides.

However, despite this surface realism, it soon becomes obvious that his laconic descriptions are not truly realistic. A true realist is prolix and indulges in long and minute inventories of external reality based on careful observations methodically recorded in notebooks, for he always carries a notebook in his pocket to collect so-called true facts. Thus Arnold Bennett after walking along the Thames noted: "I passed 68 gulls sitting on the railings. . . ." [6] The idea of counting gulls while taking a walk would have made Sherwood Anderson laugh. "The writer with a notebook in his hand," he noted in a letter, "is always a bad workman, a man who distrusts his imagination." [7]

Anyway, though he described the surface of life with impartiality and candor, Sherwood Anderson wanted above all to go beyond it, as he said quite explicitly in dedicating *Winesburg, Ohio,* to his mother:

> To the memory of my mother, Emma Smith Anderson, whose keen observations on the life about her first awoke in me the hunger to see beneath the surface of lives, this book is dedicated.

He attributes the very same hunger to George Willard, the central hero of the book:

> Half frightened and yet fascinated by the light burning in the eyes of the hideous old man, George Willard listened, afire with curiosity. . . . When in the gathering darkness, he could no longer see the purple, bloated face and the burning eyes, a curious fancy came to him. . . . In the darkness the young reporter found himself imagining that he sat on the railroad ties beside a comely young man with black hair and black shining eyes. . . ." [8]

Thus, where a true realist would have seen nothing but a hideous and dirty old man, George-Willard-Anderson "imagines" that the old telegraph operator has become "a comely young man with black hair and black shining eyes." The railroad ties remain unchanged, but the character has undergone a strange transmutation from vile lead into precious gold.

Realism merely provides Sherwood Anderson with a basis on which to build the almost fantastic stories of his grotesques. Lionel Trilling missed the point when he protested against the lack of reality of his fiction, against what he called "a pretty inadequate representation of reality." "In Anderson's world," he said, "there are many emotions, or rather many instances of a few emotions, but there are few sights, sounds, and smells, very little of the stuff of reality." [9] Actuality was merely a springboard for Anderson's imagination. He was not interested in what realists rather naïvely call truth. At the very beginning of his foreword to *Tar,* he unequivocally declared: "I have a confession to make. I am a story teller telling a story and cannot be expected to tell the truth. Truth is impossible to me. . . ." [10] And in his "Note on Realism," he added: "No man can quite make himself a camera. Even the most realistic worker pays some tribute to what is called 'art.' Where does representation end and art begin? The location of the line is often as confusing to practicing artists as it is to the public." [11]

So, contrary to what Trilling claimed in another part of his essay, Sherwood Anderson very clearly realized that art is not necessarily synonymous with artifice and must not therefore be avoided at all costs. He was fully aware that he was an artist himself whenever he let his imagination interfere with, and distort, reality—which happened most of the time when he was telling stories. He considered this an inevitable process and even a desirable one. For to his mind, realism, the mere reproduction of reality, must not be an end in itself, but only a means to an end. To what end?

By and large he was not particularly interested in banal everyday occurrences. He said himself in *A Story Teller's Story:* "I have come to think that the true history of life is but a story of comments. It is only at rare moments that we live." [12] Consequently, he felt he must select and give only a discontinuous image of life, throwing into relief those intense crucial moments when we cease to have standard reactions and fully become ourselves. He was therefore less interested in his characters' everyday gestures and daily experiences than in their dark and secret life, and that is why *Winesburg, Ohio,* is largely set in twilight or obscurity, as if the characters dared to become or express themselves only under cover of darkness, when sheltered by night. It is then that they can let out what they usually keep hidden or unexpressed for fear of being laughed at or even punished by the community in which they live. What is thus brought to the surface is often some neurosis of sexual origin, but, although some of them display abnormal tendencies— homosexuality in the case of Wing Biddlebaum, nymphomania in the case of Mrs. Willard before her marriage, exhibitionism in the case of Alice Hindman, who cannot resist the impulse to go out naked into the street, etc.—Sherwood Anderson was not interested in abnormal characters for their own sake. He was not a disciple of Freud. Though sex is a powerful urge in his characters' lives, it is never really an obsession. Their world is not ruled over by an all-pervasive *libido.* Moreover, Sherwood Anderson does not explore their minds in order to find out how they could best get readjusted to society, for he regards the individual as more precious than society and society as something dull and sterile.

He was not a sexual realist, either. Though frank about sexual matters, he remains very discreet on the whole. In "Nobody Knows," we do not know, either, for he has censored the description of George Willard's intercourse with Louise Trunnion. All we get is a line of suspension points. But what his characters crave is less the satisfaction of a physical need than the fulfilment of a mysterious spiritual hunger, which psychoanalysts would no doubt interpret in terms of sexual love, but which he refuses for his part to consider in such a crude light. To him it is something ethereal and hardly expressible, and it is this hunger for love that he wants to express above all. What matters in his stories is not what he actually describes in a more or less realistic manner, but what he suggests and leaves unsaid. He has described his method himself in terms of painting in "Loneliness":

> When a picture he [Enoch Robinson, the hero of the story] had painted was under discussion, he wanted to burst out with something like this: "You don't get the point," he wanted to explain; "the picture you see doesn't consist of the

things you see and say words about. There is something else, something you don't see at all, something you are not intended to see. Look at this one over here. . . . The dark spot by the road that you might not notice at all is, you see, the beginning of everything. There is a clump of elders there . . . and in among the elders there is something hidden. It is a woman, that's what it is. She has been thrown from a horse and the horse has run away out of sight. . . . It's a woman you see, that's what it is! It's a woman and, oh, she is lovely! She is hurt and suffering but she makes no sound. . . . She lies quite still, white and still, and the beauty comes out from her and spreads over everything. . . . I didn't try to paint the woman, of course. She is too beautiful to be painted.[13]

This passage gives us a key to Sherwood Anderson's aesthetics. What counts in *Winesburg, Ohio,* is not George Willard or the grotesques who people the village, but the love which they hide in their hearts, something *beyond* appearances. The grotesques in the book are not merely what they seem to be. Nothing in Winesburg really is what it seems to be. The hands of Wing Biddlebaum are not merely human hands, but "the piston-rods of his machinery of expression" or "the wings of an imprisoned bird." Further on, they are metamorphosed into "fluttering pennants of promise," closely akin to Whitman's "pennants of joy" in "Song of the Open Road" (paragraph 7, l. 5) and "The Sleepers" (paragraph 1, l. 41).

Exterior resemblances do not count, but only the meaning, the secret life of things. Such images have very little plastic value. They are not intended to describe the outside, but to suggest the inside of things. When he was working at *The Triumph of the Egg,* Sherwood Anderson jotted down in a notebook: "I do not intend to lift you *out of* yourself. What I intend is to lift you *into* yourself." [14] No wonder he cried out in April 1922 in a letter to a friend: "Down with realism! A bas naturalism! Up with fantasy!" [15]

Contrary to what contemporary reviewers thought, then, "realism" is not the term which must be applied to Sherwood Anderson's art. Two other words would be more appropriate, though he never used them himself: symbolism and expressionism.

There are indeed other symbolic hands in *Winesburg, Ohio,* besides the restless hands of Wing Biddlebaum—those of Dr. Reefy: "The knuckles of the Doctor's hands," Sherwood Anderson tells us, "were extraordinarily large. When the hands were closed, they looked like clusters of unpainted wooden balls as large as walnuts fastened together by steel rods." (As if they had been painted by Fernand Léger.) Later, Sherwood Anderson compares them to the gnarled, twisted apples left by the pickers in an orchard, and he adds: "Only the few know the sweetness of the twisted apples." This is obviously an elder bush, and we must look for the woman hidden in the middle of it.

Apparently hands had always obsessed Sherwood Anderson. The obsession dated back to his childhood, for in *Tar* he confessed: "People's hands, rooms in houses, the faces of fields were things the child did not forget: the old carpenter had short stumpy fingers. The nails were black and broken. The fingers of the doctor were, like his mother's, rather long." [16] Once, during a serious illness, he had a nightmare: "Things that should be small became large, things that should remain large, became small. Often Tar's own hands, white and small, seemed to leave his arms and float away. They floated away over the tops of the trees seen through the window and almost disappeared into the sky." [17] But young Tar-Anderson was especially impressed by his mother's hands: "The slender, long, work-roughened fingers of Tar's mother fascinated him. He remembered them clearly long afterward, when her figure began to grow dim in his mind. It may have been the memory of his mother's hands that made him think so much about other people's hands. With their hands, young lovers touched each other tenderly, painters spent a long lifetime training the hands to follow the dictates of their fancies, men in workshops grasped tools with their hands. Hands young and strong, boneless soft hands at the ends of arms of boneless soft men, hands of fighters—knocking other men down—the steady quiet hands of railroad engineers at the throttles of huge engines, soft hands creeping toward bodies in the night, hands beginning to age, to tremble, the hands of a mother that touch the babe, the hands of a mother remembered clearly, the hands of a father forgotten." [18] (This list reads almost like one of Whitman's catalogues.)

Hands are thus charged with meaning for Sherwood Anderson, and he discloses what they mean to him incidentally, almost accidentally toward the end of *Winesburg, Ohio,* when, referring to George Willard's hands, he says: "With all his heart he wants to come close to some other human, touch someone with his hands, be touched by the hand of another." [19] Hands thus mean communication and communion between men. It is through them that the love of one man for another can flow and that is why they loom so large in Sherwood Anderson's internal universe.

In the same way, many unobtrusive details in Sherwood Anderson's fiction have a meaning and are not mere inanimate stage properties. Bedrooms suggest the isolation of the individual who feels "choked and walled-in by life in [an] apartment." The church tower in which in the Reverend Hartman meditates and prays alone at night symbolizes a still greater degree of isolation. The repressed and unsatisfied craving for love of the inhabitants of Winesburg is again and again suggested by words like "hunger" or its corollary "to feed." All these words or images project us beyond appearances into a world where everything is different and mysterious. There are constant correspondences between the so-called real world and the spiritual world of love which it hides. Some of these images are quite transparent, but others are like thick clumps of elders on the roadside. They either fail to attract our attention because they seem so banal, or, if they somehow arrest us, we cannot pierce their mystery.

So, though we may not notice it, in "The Strength of God," the Reverend Curtis Hartman's Bible is at first open on his desk and is the source from which he draws his inspiration for the sermon he is writing. Later, when he is assailed by temptation, the Bible is still there, but he does not even look at it. When he finally triumphs over temptation, it falls from his desk with a great clatter. All these are not mere realistic notations intended to give the reader a true picture of a minister's environment. They are much more than that. They are meant to illustrate the fact that "the strength of God," which originally emanated from the Bible, in the last scene, ironically enough, reaches the Reverend Hartman through the very temptation which very nearly destroyed him, and at that time the Bible is no longer of any use to him.

The same story contains more mysterious details. In the minister's study, at the top of the bell tower of his church, there is a stained glass window "showing the Christ laying his hand on the head of a child." When the Reverend Hartman discovers that from this window he can see a woman lying in bed and smoking in the upper room of the house across the street, he breaks one of the little leaded panes of the window the better to watch her without running the risk of being seen himself. Now, it happens that the broken piece of glass "just nipped off the bare heel of the boy standing motionless and looking with rapt eyes into the face of Christ." Why should it be the heel of the boy? Sherwood Anderson, of course, does not tell us. It is up to us to guess, up to us to remember Genesis III: 15, where the Lord curses the serpent in the following words: "And I will put enmity between thee and the woman, and between thy seed and her seed: it shall bruise thy head and thou shalt bruise his heel."

The heel thus stands for man's vulnerability to evil. It is our heel that the serpent stings and through our heel that evil invades us. It is natural therefore that evil thoughts should enter the minister's mind through the hole in the young boy's heel. But one night, just as the Reverend Hartman is about to yield to sinful thoughts, he catches sight of the woman kneeling on her bed and praying, looking exactly like the boy on the stained glass window. In short, he finds innocence where he expected to find sin. Purity is made whole again, and the minister, after smashing the window with his fist, goes out crying: "I have found the light. . . . God has manifested himself in the body of a woman."

Other episodes resist analysis. Thus in "Mother," Sherwood Anderson tells us how George Willard's mother often observed the feud between the baker and a neighbor's gray cat. The cat would creep into the bakery and presently emerge chased by the baker, who swore and hurled at the cat everything he could lay his hands on, but the cat always came back. What did it mean? It is difficult to tell, and yet it *is* intended to mean something, for whenever Mrs. Willard witnessed the scene, it made her break into sobs, because, Sherwood Anderson tells us, "it seemed like a rehearsal of her own life, terrible in its vividness." [20]

Thus we do not always find the woman hidden away among the

elders, but it does not matter, for what counts is not the precise meaning of this or that detail, but the light diffused through the sky over the clump of elders. We find once more here "the light that never was on sea or land," the light projected over reality by the author's imagination, "the Poet's dream." [21]

Sherwood Anderson's tales are so many meditations on life in the form of images. They express, on the one hand, his conviction that life is absurd and, on the other hand, the love for all that lives, which he cannot help experiencing, as he says quite explicitly toward the end of *Winesburg, Ohio,* in "Sophistication": "One shudders at the thought of the meaninglessness of life, while at the same instant . . . one loves life so intensely that tears come into the eyes." Consequently, he is interested in his characters from a metaphysical or religious rather than a psychological or social point of view. In his eyes, they symbolized that baffling, impenetrable mystery of life which fascinated him. The spectacle of even the most humble life going on about him sometimes stirred intense emotions and nearly intoxicated him. In *A Story Teller's Story,* he has told how one day, through his study window, he saw a man picking potato bugs while his wife was scolding him for having forgotten to buy sugar. "I was unconscious," he wrote, "of a dinner being put on a table downstairs in my house, unconscious of any need of food: A man and a woman in a garden had become the center of a universe about which it seemed to me I might think and feel in joy and wonder forever." [22]

It is this sense of wonder, this intense perception of the fundamental beauty and preciousness of life despite its apparent chaos and occasional repulsiveness, that Sherwood Anderson tried passionately to express and communicate. We find ourselves here at the very heart of his aesthetics, in the thick of the elder bush. And it is rather dark there, for Sherwood Anderson has provided very little light to help the investigator. Whenever he attempted to define his intentions in intellectual terms, he expressed himself in such fuzzy language that one has to translate it, as it were, to make it intelligible. Thus, one day he confided to a friend: "I presume that we all who begin the practice of an art begin out of a great hunger for order." (That is, we all want to build up a coherent representation of the world.) And he went on: "We want brought into consciousness something that is always there but that gets terribly lost." (That is, a presence which we apprehend through insight rather than through our senses.) He gave a concrete example of what he meant: "I am walking on a country road and there is a man on a hillside plowing. There is something nice, almost beautiful, in a man striding at the plow handles, in the beast pulling, in the earth rolling back from the plow, in the newly turned earth below and in the sky above." [23] (He evinces here a cosmic sense and an esemplastic power worthy of Whitman.)

Like a true romantic artist he despised form: "You see, I have the belief that in this matter of form, it is largely a matter of depth of feeling. How deeply do you feel it? Feel it deeply enough and you will be torn inside and driven on until form comes." [24] It is all a matter of inspiration. Nothing else really counts.

Actually, though "driven on" and "torn inside" to the point of abandoning his business and his family in order to devote himself wholly to his art, he was not at all indifferent to or unaware of the technical aspects of storytelling. For all his dash and passion, he was, in his own way, a conscious and conscientious artist. He did not write off his stories at one sitting, but often rewrote them several times. He thus gradually and gropingly evolved his own medium. When he started writing, it was the fashion to compose realistic stories, and so he wrote some like everyone else, but he soon developed his own form of realism by combining realistic descriptions with more or less elaborate symbolic images, and the result was sometimes quite close to expressionism.

*Ex*pressionism essentially consists in *ex*teriorizing subjective *im*pressions by *ex*aggerating certain aspects of *ex*ternal reality. Now this is precisely what Sherwood Anderson does in some of his stories where we can observe the abnormal predominance of some detail which obviously obsesses him. Hands, for instance, keep fluttering in the story which bears this title and in which we see more hands than faces.

At other times, the process of distortion is subtler. Thus, at the beginning of "Departure," the last story in *Winesburg, Ohio,* the second sentence of the first paragraph calls up a spring landscape full of hope and promise, but the very next sentence projects us into autumn among winged maple seeds whirling crazily about.

This detail seems quite irrelevant; it is even in direct contradiction with the date of the story and the rest of the setting; it has no realistic value whatever, but it is meant to suggest the underlying sadness of George Willard's departure, the erratic course of life, the absurdity of existence. (Incidentally, this telescoping of inconsistent details is a device Virginia Woolf also used occasionally.)

Sherwood Anderson's ultimate aim was to communicate moods rather than tell stories. His subjects were "moments," as he said, "revelations," sudden intuitions provoked by some more or less banal incident. So he needed no plot and never had enough matter for a novel. Even in the story called "Adventure," in fact, nothing really happens in spite of the promise of the title. His was a world of contemplation rather than action. And, in this connection, it must be noted that nobody, or hardly anybody, kills or gets killed in his stories. Even Wash Williams does not really kill his mother-in-law for all his passion; she rather anticlimactically dies of a fever one month after he has beaten her with a chair. How different from the worlds of Faulkner or Hemingway and all their successors! His stories, thus, are rather sketches than stories proper. Rather than fiction, they are lyric poetry in the form of fiction. Each of them is a poetic epiphany in the course of which we are suddenly brought into contact with the inexpressible mystery of life. At least Sherwood Anderson tries to make us feel it or get a glimpse of it. Unfortunately, he sometimes fails. The "new looseness" [25] on which he counted so much and which was to free him from the shackles of convention occasionally proved to be a hindrance rather than a help. There are times when the clumps of elders are so thick and so dark that it becomes quite impossible to see the woman hidden among them or even suspect that there can be one there.

She is there just the same, unattainable, but almost within reach—like Emerson's oversoul.

Notes

1. "A New Novelist," in *Horizons* (New York: Huebsch, 1918), pp. 50-56.
2. See William L. Phillips, "How Sherwood Anderson Wrote *Winesburg, Ohio,*" *American Literature,* vol. 23 (March 1951), pp. 7-30.

3. "Queer," *Winesburg, Ohio,* ed. by John H. Ferres (New York: Viking Critical Edition, 1966), pp. 190-91.
4. *Tar* (New York: Boni & Liveright, 1926), p. 6.
5. *Winesburg, Ohio,* op. cit., p. 32.
6. Quoted from his *Journal* by Reginald Pound in *Arnold Bennett* (London: W. Heinemann, 1952), p. 224. Bennett believed in *Mental Efficiency* and wrote a book about it.
7. "The Sherwood Anderson Papers," *Newberry Library Bulletin,* 2nd Series, No. 2 (Dec., 1948), p. 70.
8. "Respectability," *Winesburg, Ohio,* op. cit., pp. 124-25.
9. Ibid., pp. 458, 461-62.
10 *Tar,* p. ix.
11. See *The Sherwood Anderson Reader,* ed. by Paul Rosenfeld (Boston: Houghton Mifflin, 1947), p. 343.
12. *A Story Teller's Story* (New York: Grove Press, n.d.), p. 406.
13. *Winesburg, Ohio,* op. cit., pp. 169-70. Curiously enough, in no. 12 of *La Révolution Surréaliste* for December 15, 1929, there is a photo-montage by René Magritte, the Belgian surrealist painter, illustrating the same idea. In the center one sees the picture of a naked woman; above her is written: "Je ne vois pas la" and under her: "cachée dans la forêt," i.e., "I do not see [the naked woman] hidden in the forest." This central motif is framed by a series of photographs showing a number of surrealist writers with their eyes closed. Was it a borrowing from *Winesburg, Ohio* or the result of a coincidence? It is impossible to tell.
14. *Sherwood Anderson's Notebook* (New York: Boni & Liveright, 1926).
15. This friend was Gilbert Seldes.
16. *Tar,* p. 71.
17. Ibid., pp. 104-5.
18. Ibid., p. 276.
19. "Sophistication," *Winesburg, Ohio,* op. cit., p. 235.
20. "Mother," ibid., p. 41.
21. See William Wordsworth, "Peele Castle," *Poetical Works* (London: Oxford University Press, 1913), p. 578, ll. 15-16.
22. *A Story Teller's Story,* op. cit., p. 317.
23. See Norman Holmes Pearson, "Anderson and the New Puritanism," *Newberry Library Bulletin,* 2nd Series, no. 2 (December 1948), p. 57.
24. Ibid.
25. By this he meant his indifference to plot and dramatic structure.

10.

Hemingway, or "Sartor Resartus" Once More

Though history never quite repeats itself, the same causes to a large extent produce the same effects and thus, other things being equal, the Napoleonic wars and the so-called Great War both resulted in the same general collapse of political, moral, religious, and aesthetic structures, brought about the same crash of commonly accepted values, and created the same spiritual vacuum. Carlyle and Bernanos, Francis Scott Fitzgerald and Musset, Byron and Hemingway were all equally "enfants du siècle," "children of the century." They all suffered from the same "mal du siècle." "Tout était vide," [1] "everything was empty," Musset complained, and, a hundred years later, Scott Fitzgerald's "sad young men" echoed his complaint and similarly lamented because they found "all Gods dead, all wars fought, all faiths in man shaken." [2] They were, as he also said, "cynical rather than revolutionary, tired of great causes." [3] Some of them were so tired and sick to nausea that they committed suicide. Harry Crosby in particular, who had come to Europe believing that "God [had] ordained this war . . . and when it's over the world will be a finer, cleaner, and squarer place." [4] He served as an ambulance driver like E. E. Cummings,

John Dos Passos, and Hemingway, but on the French, not on "the picturesque front," [5] and he never succeeded in forgetting the horrors he had seen. He felt so miserable in the Waste Land of the postwar world that, though immensely rich and in principle happily married, he committed suicide in 1929.

It was indeed a "lost generation" in more senses than one. Yet, Hemingway among others survived the Great War for over forty years and, after appearing as the cynical and disillusioned Byron of the twentieth century, ultimately turned into a new "teacher of athletes" and a "professeur d'énergie" à la Barrès. A rather surprising change and a very spectacular recovery, which we can follow step by step in his works, since his novels make up an interminable *Bildungsroman* whose hero is always himself. In his early short stories he offers us a portrait of the artist as a boy and a young man, perhaps symbolically called Nick Adams, a combination of Nick, the Devil, and Adam or prelapsarian innocence in the Garden of Eden. Frederick Henry, Jake Barnes, Harry Morgan, Robert Jordan, Colonel Cantwell, Santiago, the Old Man, and Thomas Hudson, the painter, are all avatars of himself. They grow old with him—whereas the heroines, on the contrary, remain eternally young. His protagonists were projections of himself as he would have liked to be—and to some extent really was, at least potentially. Their adventures, which he partly lived and partly "invented truly," to borrow his own phrase, constitute, as it were, *The Education of Nick Adams,* a fascinating record of his experiences, a lifelong *Erlebnis,* rather than a piece of intellectual history like *The Education of Henry Adams.* His fiction , in other words, provides us with a graph of his evolution from innocence to experience through despair and cynicism, and the hard-won equilibrium of his middle years up to the apparent serenity of his old age. His life and his works were carried away by a dialectical movement which, to some extent, parallels the movement of *Sartor Resartus,* although less dramatically and with a less resounding "everlasting yea." After the "idyllic" passage of youth, we get under way and witness the "sorrows" of Frederick, visit the "Centre of Indifference," and eventually reach (or hear) the "everlasting no." It is indispensable to distinguish these various stages for the sake of logic and clarity, though, of course they sometimes overlap chronologically.

"Happy season of childhood!" exclaims Teufelsdröckh.[6] It is hard to say whether Hemingway's childhood was happy, but it certainly was a period of enforced innocence. He was born at Oak Park in the suburbs of Chicago, but there was then almost a difference in kind between the two places. Chicago was Hell and Oak Park a modern—and improved—version of the Garden of Eden, for, as the saying was, it was the place where the saloons stopped and the churches began. Both of Hemingway's parents were ardently religious, and one of his paternal uncles was a missionary in China. His mother was a devout Episcopalian and his father a stern Congregationalist and a strict disciplinarian. For him, right was right and wrong was wrong. There were no half measures. When young Ernest used coarse language, he was sent upstairs to wash his mouth with toilet soap. Hemingway senior believed that dancing, card playing, and gambling were wrong, and he absolutely disapproved of smoking and drinking alcoholic beverages. Young Ernest thus spent an artificially sheltered childhood in a vice-proof, teetotaling community where virtue and high moral ideals were compulsory. The only times when he had a chance to live a more natural and less restrained life were during the summer holidays, when he could fish and shoot and swim like a young savage "up in Michigan." In Oak Park, he had no choice but to be a "clean young American," a God-fearing young man, completely cut off from reality, pent-up in the closest approximation to the American dream that could then be found in the United States.

This phase of idyllic innocence could not last forever. It ended rather abruptly when, after serving a six months' apprenticeship as a cub reporter on the staff of the Kansas City *Star,* Hemingway suddenly found himself right in the middle of World War I on the Italian front, a new innocent abroad whose untried idealism was unexpectedly confronted with the sordid reality of war. "I was an awful dope when I went to the last war," he was to say later on, "I can remember just thinking that we were the home team and the Austrians were the visiting team." [7] He had enlisted as a volunteer ambulance driver, because he wanted to watch the game. And at first he was delighted. He arrived in Paris just as the city was being bombarded by Big Bertha and, as soon as a shell blew up, he took a taxi and rushed to the scene to contemplate the damage. In

Milan, he was equally lucky. A big munitions-factory exploded when he got there and he had to help pick up the dead—mostly women—and gather shapeless human fragments from trees and barbed wire fences. This baptism of war, for all his bravado, gave him a considerable shock. He got over it at the time, but soon made other disconcerting discoveries—notably that women are not necessarily angels and soldiers generally are no choirboys. There were houses of ill repute behind the front to bolster up the morale of the troops. Far from being outlawed, they were quasi-official institutions: some were intended for officers and others for enlisted men. Frederick Henry occasionally visited them, but, when he came back, Rinaldi taunted him: "I know you are the fine good Anglo-Saxon boy, I know. You are the remorse boy, I know. I will wait till I see the Anglo-Saxon brushing away harlotry with a toothbrush." [8] But Anglo-Saxon hygiene was powerless to obliterate Latin—or human—corruption. All the illusions of the young midwestern innocent were destroyed in quick succession. Hemingway presently found out that modern armies were not made up of heroes, but of unwilling civilians caught in the cogs of a ruthless machine and compelled to go to the front lines whether they liked it or not. If they resisted, they were shot by the military police. The only way out was a self-inflicted wound, and many tried it with various degrees of ingenuity and success. Gallantry did not exist. The bravest troops, the Alpini, the Bersaglieri, had been known to run away. "There is nothing worse than war," Passini concludes in *A Farewell to Arms*.[9] Far from ennobling, it debases everything it touches.

This direct experience of the evils of war à la Goya was soon completed by a personal encounter with death. In July 1918, at Fossalta di Piave, while engaged in the rather unheroic occupation of eating a piece of cheese, Hemingway was very severely wounded by an Austrian shell and machine-gun fire, and nearly killed. He has recounted it in *A Farewell to Arms:* ". . . there was a flash, as a blast-furnace door is swung open, and a roar that started white and went red and on and on in a rushing wind. I tried to breathe but my breath would not come and I felt myself rush bodily out of myself and out and out and all the time bodily in the wind. I went out swiftly, all of myself and I knew I was dead and that it had all been a mistake to think you just died. Then I floated, and instead of going on I felt myself slide back. I breathed and I was back." [10]

This was an ambiguous experience. On the one hand, Hemingway very proudly found out that he could "take it" as well as anyone else: he had been initiated and—without any irony—had received "the red badge of courage." But, on the other hand, he had also made the startling discovery that he was mortal. "When you go to war as a boy," he wrote in 1942, "you have a great illusion of immortality. Other people can get killed, not you. It can happen to other people; but not to you. Then when you are badly wounded the first time you lose that illusion and you know it can happen to you. After being severely wounded two weeks before my nineteenth birthday I had a bad time. . . ." [11] Until then death had been an abstraction to him, now it was a reality, and a frightening and horrible reality at that, which gave him nightmares and insomnia to such an extent that for weeks and even months afterward he could not go to sleep without a light in his room.

When he returned to the United States in 1919, he was a much sobered and very disillusioned young man. Though feted at first as a war hero by his home town, he did not feel at home at all. He was unable to adjust himself to a society whose principles he now regarded as a mere sham. His parents took it for granted that after a brief respite he could carry on as if nothing had happened. But he could not bring himself to do it. Like Krebs, the hero of "Soldier's Home," he felt "angry," "sick and vaguely nauseated," and his parents reacted very much like those of Krebs. "Unless you, my son Ernest, come to yourself; cease your lazy loafing and pleasure-seeking . . . and neglecting your duties to God, and your Savior, Jesus Christ . . . there is nothing for you but bankruptcy—you have overdrawn," [12] his mother wrote to him. So, like Krebs, he decided to run away. At the earliest opportunity, he turned his back on puritan America, prohibition, moral purity, the myth of success, and all the rest of it, and left for Paris.

There, although outwardly happy and hard at work, he went through his "centre of indifference," his nihilistic period. Every day was not a moveable feast. More than once, in the solitude of his "mansarde" (garret) on rue du Cardinal Lemoine, he must have been licking his psychic wounds far from the crowd of his noisy and unthinking fellow expatriates. The war which he had just gone through and which still lingered in the Balkans and Turkey had debased all the things he believed in. As he wrote in *A Farewell to Arms:* "I was always embarrassed by the words sacred, glorious and sacrifice and the expression in vain. We had heard them, sometimes standing in the rain almost out of earshot, so that only the shouted words came through, and had read them on proclamations that were slapped up by bill posters over other proclamations . . . and I had seen nothing sacred, and the things that were glorious had no glory and the sacrifices were like the stockyards at Chicago if nothing was done with the meat except to bury it . . . finally only the names of places had dignity. . . . Abstract words such as glory, courage, or hallow were obscene beside the concrete names of villages, the numbers of roads, the names of rivers." [13] All the traditional values had thus become devalued and were just as worthless as German currency. As John Peale Bishop, one of Hemingway's exact contemporaries and the prototype of Tom d'Invilliers in *This Side of Paradise,* noted: "The most tragic thing about the war was not that it made so many dead men, but that it destroyed the tragedy of death. Not only did the young suffer in the war, but every abstraction that would have sustained and given dignity to their suffering. The war made the traditional morality unacceptable . . . so that at its end, the survivors were left to face, as they could, a world without values." [14]

This kind of disillusionment was general. In France a slightly older veteran, Georges Bernanos, reached much the same conclusion: ". . . we were so sick of phoney blah, of Right and Justice and Morale, that we didn't know any more how to speak to kids; we didn't dare any more; it seemed to us we were reciting by heart articles from the Military Gazette, passed by the censor. My foot!" [15]

The bottom seemed to have dropped out of everything. The world was empty, life absurd and meaningless, since the war had reduced men to the condition of passive, expendable things herded en masse into the vast slaughterhouses of the western world. The individual felt like Frederick Henry, "lonely and empty," [16] alienated from the society into which he happened to be born, a stranger, in short. Even the word "soul" had lost its meaning and sounded obscene and dirty.[17] "I do not know about the soul," says Frederick Henry. "We none of us knows," answers his interlocutor, Count Greffi, and this was nearly the only occasion when Hemingway ever used the word "soul" in his fiction.[18] His characters are men and women without souls. They are more ashamed of their souls than of their bodies. He wrote almost as if the word had become completely obsolete.

And no wonder, since the lost generation practically lived in a godless world—very much like the one which Carlyle described in *Sartor Resartus: "Aus der Ewigkeit,zu der Ewigkeit hin:* from Eternity, onwards to Eternity! These are Apparitions: what else? Are they not souls rendered visible: in Bodies, that took shape and will lose it, melting into air?" [19] In the same way, Hemingway's characters are only very provisionally staying in "a clean well-lighted place," but they will sooner or later be engulfed forever in nothingness. As the Spanish waiter philosophizes in "A Clean Well-Lighted Place": "What did he fear? . . . It was a nothing that he knew too well. It was all a nothing and a man was nothing too. It was only that and light was all it needed and a certain closeness and order. Some lived in it and never felt it but he knew it all was nada y pues nada y pues nada." He goes on parodying the Lord's Prayer: "Our nada who art in nada, nada be thy name, thy Kingdom nada, thy will be nada in nada as it is in nada. Give us this nada our daily nada and nada us our nada as we nada our nadas and nada us not into nada but deliver us from nada y pues nada." [20] It is quite likely that Hemingway was here playing on the words nada and dada, and wanted to suggest by this almost nonsensical use of the Spanish word for "nothing" that his own brand of nihilism was just as desolate and despairing as that of Tristan Tzara and all the other dadaists.

At this point Hemingway's position is fundamentally identical with that of the Ecclesiast: "All is vanity. . . . One generation passeth away, and another generation cometh, but the earth abideth for ever. The sun also ariseth. . . ." [21] *The Sun Also Rises* and Jake Barnes and Lady Brett Ashley and the others strut and fret their hour upon the stage and then are heard no more, to take up the words that Macbeth used when he realized his delusion. The situation of man in the Waste Land of the postwar world was desperate too. If you did not share the faith of the priest from the Abruzzi, the only sensible thing to do was to destroy yourself like Rinaldi by drinking too much and / or making love indiscriminately and catching syphilis—"self-destruction day by day," [22] Rinaldi called it.

Hemingway, however, found another way out, since he survived the Great War until 1961. Like Dr. Teufelsdröckh, he could probably have said: "From Suicide a certain after shine *(Nachschein)* of Christianity withheld me." [23] After touching the bottom, he gave a kick and rose to the surface again. He could not live interminably in a spiritual vacuum. Absolute nihilism is an untenable position. In a way, as Edgar Johnson has pointed out, his scepticism of the immediate postwar years, other things being equal, corresponds to Descartes's provisional doubt, which he used as "a stage preparatory to a new departure," [24] as a *tabula rasa* on which to build a truer and more harmonious conception of life.

The first remedies which Hemingway applied to his trauma were mere anaesthetics. All abstractions being debased, Thought with a capital *T* having led to disaster,[25] only concrete things, only the physical world mattered. "I lay down on the bed and tried to stop from thinking,[26] said Frederick Henry, and he added: "I was not made to think. I was made to eat. My God, yes. Eat and drink and sleep with Catherine." [27] In other words, if you wanted to save yourself, there was only one thing for you to do: you must become wholly engrossed in concrete, material activities. Hemingway has explained this strategy in particular in "Big Two-Hearted River." In doing so, he was quite literally following the advice of the Ecclesiast: "There is nothing better for a man than that he should eat and drink, and that he should make his soul enjoy good in his labour." [28] This is why he became a connoisseur of food and wines and alcoholic drinks of all kinds. In fact, his characters enjoy drinking so much and so convincingly that it is impossible to read his books without feeling thirsty. And they drink so often and at such regular intervals that it gives the reader a sense of duration. Alcohol in Hemingway's novels serves the same purpose as a clepsydra or water clock. It reminds us of the flight of time. The drinks taken by the characters are a kind of temporal punctuation, whereas hunting and fishing become the supreme diversion, especially in

Green Hills of Africa, which culminates in a sort of quest for the unicorn in the form of a perfect kudu.

Thus Hemingway's instinctive, visceral reaction after his European ordeal was to cling to life, to imbibe it greedily through all his senses. Life is indeed better than nothing in his eyes. However disappointing, tragic, and unsatisfactory the form of existence to which we are condemned here below may be, it is infinitely better than the terrible nothingness in which we are doomed sooner or later to be engulfed. "Do you value life?" asks Count Greffi. "Yes," answers Frederick. "So do I," says Count Greffi, "because it is all I have." [29]

But Hemingway and his heroes soon realized that this desperate hedonism, this deliberate epicureanism did not suffice. The pleasures of the flesh or the satisfaction you derive from a well-done job can only be palliatives or sedatives, pastimes in the Pascalian sense of the word, drugs, "opiums of the people," to use Karl Marx's phrase. This is the discovery which Frazer, the writer in "The Gambler, the Nun and the Radio," is supposed to make while staying in the hospital: "Yes, and music is the opium of the people. Old Mount-to-the-head [i.e., Karl Marx] had not thought of that. . . . But drink was a sovereign opium of the people, oh, an excellent opium. Although some people prefer the radio, another opium of the people, a cheap one he had just been using. . . ."

But no one can live on *panem et circenses* alone. As the Ecclesiast had already found out: "To every thing there is a season, and a time to every purpose under the heaven. A time to kill and a time to heal; a time to break down and a time to build up." [30] Remembering his wartime emotions in tranquillity, Hemingway discovered that war, in fact, does not destroy everything. Like an acid it corrodes and removes all that is soft and unprotected and thus gives a stronger relief to what remains. It etches, as it were, the men who survive its contact. It is a touchstone and a test. It tries your mettle. It gives you a chance to find out whether you can look death in the face or not. It teaches you how to control fear—all fear being in the last analysis the fear of death. Courage, then, ceases to be an abstract word. It becomes a reality, one of the few realities that count—which you can learn only through experience. So those who have gone through the ordeal of war, even if they have been scorched and partly broken, are almost different in kind from their fellow men. They are even stronger in the places where they were originally broken. They have been initiated into the quasi-secret society of those who know what life really means and is. They belong to "El Ordine Militar, Nobile y Esperituoso de los Caballeros de Brusadelli," founded by Colonel Cantwell. They are natural aristocrats regardless of their social origins. The Gran Maestro is the headwaiter of the Gritti Hotel in Venice and he is the Italian counterpart, one World War later, of the manager of the Hotel Montoya in Pamplona in *The Sun Also Rises*. Of course Jake Barnes belongs to it and so do Pilar, that pillar of strength, Count Mippipopoulos, Kandisky, the Austrian hunter in *Green Hills of Africa*, and Santiago, the old man of the sea. On the contrary, Robert Cohn, for all his physical bravery and skill at boxing, will forever remain an outsider, "indignus entrare in nostro docto corpore," because he has never been to war,[31] just as Sherwood Anderson and Gertrude Stein were for the same reason forever disqualified from treating certain essential subjects in Hemingway's opinion.[32]

All the veterans of foreign wars who appear in Hemingway's fiction are united by a common belief in an unwritten code. They are morally and physically very tough. They can take it. They keep a stiff upper lip. They grin and bear it. They refuse to discuss their own emotions and despise loquacious swaggerers like Robert Cohn. They hate gushing. They believe in self-control and self-imposed discipline. They have reached true wisdom in the etymological meaning of the word "wisdom." They are those who know—who know that they are mortal and that sooner or later life ends in death. They know that man—whatever he does—will sooner or later be crushed by the hostile forces which surround him and is bound to be defeated—defeated, but not vanquished, for, like Pascal, they believe in the dignity of man, "a mere reed, and the weakest that can be found on earth, but even when the universe crushes him, man is still nobler than what kills him, for he knows that he is dying, while the advantage that the universe has over him, the universe is unaware of it." [33]

Most of the values extolled by Hemingway are British sportsmen's values (he always admired the British in this respect), but they are combined with that Spanish sense of death which he has exalted in *Death in the Afternoon.* He regarded bullfighting as a ritual, a *memento mori* implicitly understood by all *aficionados,* and he contrasted the American dream of life as a perpetual pursuit of happiness and an endless flight from death, and the thought of death with the Spanish conception of life as the austere contemplation of mortality. This is a constant contrast in his fiction. It sets Harry Morgan, the heroic smuggler, against Richard Gordon, the soft intellectual, the "hollow man."

Living in conformity with this code, playing the game is a purely gratuitous activity. No reward is promised and no material gain is procured. "Winner take nothing." But the heroes feel a deep and intense satisfaction when they have behaved as they think they should have. For Hemingway this new form of stoicism is its own reward. As he hated preaching and despised didacticism, he always refused to define a new set of values explicitly or to use "big words" in his turn. But he affirmed again and again that what is moral is "what you feel good after," as even Lady Brett Ashley ultimately finds out.[34] For Jake Barnes, immorality is "things that made you disgusted afterwards," [35] and, in *Death in the Afternoon,* we are told again that "so far, about morals, I know only that what is moral is what you feel good after and what is immoral is what you feel bad after." [36]

Hemingway thus replaced the traditional abstract principles of morality by a set of subjective values passionately believed in by his heroes. These values, however were not actually new; they were often nothing but some of the old values stripped of "bunk," "debunked," as the phrase was. (It appeared during the interwar years, which was a rather significant symptom.) His moral was morals without any moralizing, in other words, a return to fundamental moral values without sententiousness or righteousness: "I hated anyone who was righteous at all, or who had ever been righteous. I hated all righteous bastards," Hemingway declared in *Green Hills of Africa.*[37] War, that manmade machine for crushing hundreds of thousands and millions of men, had taught him modesty and humility. It had taught him, among other things, that man is a puny, short-lived creature, whereas "the earth abideth for ever." The business of living is too difficult. No one can set himself up as a teacher or preacher. Everyone must work out his own salvation by himself. "Let those who want to save the world, if they can see it clear, do it," he concluded in *Death in the Afternoon*.[38]

Yet, though he had signed "a separate peace" with mankind at the end of World War I, he gradually rediscovered the meaning and value of human solidarity, that sense of human solidarity which Frederick Henry felt so instinctively that, though very seriously wounded himself, he carried one of his comrades-in-arms on his back to the nearest dressing station through the bombardment. During the depression years, distressed by the helplessness and sufferings of the veterans who were reduced to living on public charity in camps in Florida, he reached the same conclusion as Harry Morgan, the hero of *To Have and Have Not:* "No matter how, a man alone ain't got no bloody chance."[39] This tolled the knell of his rebellious individualism. The rise of fascism and nazism, the progress of a more and more dictatorial form of communism made it impossible for a man of good will—and will—to remain indifferent. So Robert Jordan, instead of denouncing "holy abstractions," like his predecessors decided to join the "crusade" against political oppression;

> That was the only word for it although it was a word that had been so worn and abused that it no longer gave its true meaning. You felt, in spite of all bureaucracy and inefficiency and party strife something that was like the feeling you expected to have and did not have after your first communion. It was a feeling of consecration to a duty toward all the oppressed of the world which would be difficult and embarrassing to talk about as a religious experience, and yet it was as authentic as when you heard Bach, or stood in Chartres Cathedral [Nick Adams here follows in Henry Adams's footsteps] or the cathedral at León and saw the lights coming through the great windows, or when you saw Mantegna, Greco, Brueghel in the Prado. It gave you a part of something you could believe in wholly, and in which you felt an absolute brotherhood.[40]

Over the centuries Hemingway then joined hands with a Christian preacher named John Donne who had proclaimed from his pulpit in St. Paul's cathedral: "No man is an Iland, intire of itself, every man is a peece of the Continent, a part of the maine . . . therefore never send to know for whom the bell tolls; It tolls for thee. . . ."

Actually, even at the height of his rebellion, Hemingway had never quite believed that man is an island entire of itself, for he never doubted Love or called it in question. He never ceased to capitalize it—mentally at least. In the middle of universal chaos it always remained intact, a permanent and indestructible value. Love is an oasis in his heroes' lives, where they can rest and forget the nada which surrounds them by transcending the limitations of time and escaping into eternity, for lust is on the level of the body, but love belongs to the realm of the spirit, as Frederick Henry finds out by passing from the one to the other. (Malraux declared that *A Farewell to Arms* was the most beautiful love story that had appeared since *The Charterhouse of Parma*.) Jake Barnes, for his part, dreams of love. Harry Morgan experiences it without expressing it. Robert Jordan both experiences and expresses it: "When I am with Maria I love her so that I feel, literally, as though I would die and I never believed in that nor thought that it could happen." [41] "What you have with Maria," he soliloquizes, "whether it lasts just through today and a part of to-morrow, or whether it lasts for a long life is the most important thing that can happen to a human being. There will always be people who say it does not exist because they cannot have it. But I tell you it is true and that you have it and that you are lucky even if you die to-morrow." [42] "I suppose it is possible to live as full a life in seventy hours as in seventy years. . . . So that if your life trades its seventy years for seventy hours I have that *value* now and I am lucky enough to know it." [43]

In Hemingway's universe, Love is thus an ideal and almost mythical value. He was in love with love and dreamed of it, but he may very well never have encountered it himself—except perhaps once with his first wife.[44] Anyway, it is worth noting that all his wives were American, whereas the women his heroes fall in love with are always submissive, absolutely passive European women. For his part, he could love them only from a distance. They were idols he worshipped without ever daring to touch them, perhaps for fear they might vanish away. Curiously enough, Marlene Dietrich was one of his lifelong idols, and, after World War II, he found another in the person of a Venetian girl called Adriana Ivancich, who served as a model for Renata, but he was less fortunate than Colonel Cantwell; his relationship with her remained purely platonic. Love as he conceived it belonged to the realm of essences, but did not exist on the level of mere existence.

He went still further, for *The Old Man and the Sea* describes an apotheosis of Love. Love ceases to be addressed to Woman only. It becomes the love of all animate and inanimate things which the old man feels for the little bird which rests for a few minutes on his boat and the big fish, his victim, and the young lions which he sees in his dreams innocently gamboling on African beaches as in the days of the Garden of Eden.

Notes

1. *La Confession d'un enfant du siècle* (Paris: G. Charpentier, 1856), Part I, chap. 2.
2. Quoted by Alfred Kazin, *On Native Grounds* (New York: Harcourt, Brace, 1942), p. 324.
3. *This Side of Paradise.*
4. Quoted by Frederick J. Hoffman, *The Twenties* (New York: Collier Books, 1962), p. 75.
5. I.e., the Italian front. Hemingway used the phrase in *A Farewell to Arms.*
6. *Sartor Resartus,* 1836, Book II, chapter 2.
7. Carlos Baker, *Ernest Hemingway—A Life Story* (New York: Scribner, 1969), p. 38.
8. *A Farewell to Arms,* chap. 25.
9. Ibid., chap. 8.
10. Ibid., chap. 9.
11. Introduction to *Men at War* (London: Fontana Books, 1966), p. 7.
12. Quoted by Carlos Baker, op. cit., p. 72.
13. *A Farewell to Arms,* chap. 27.
14. "The Missing All," quoted by John K. M. McCaffery, ed., *E. Hemingway: The Man and His Work* (Cleveland: World, 1950), p. 304. This essay originally appeared in the *Virginia Quarterly,* vol. XIII, no. 1 (Winter 1937).
15. ". . . Nous en avions tellement plein le dos des bobards à la mie de pain, et du Droit et de la Justice, et du Moral, que nous ne savions plus parler aux gosses, nous n'osions plus, nous nous faisions l'effet de réciter par coeur un article du Bulletin des Armées, visé par la censure—des clous!" *Nouvelles Littéraires,* vol. XLVII, no. 2176, (June 5, 1969), p. 11A.
16. *A Farewell to Arms,* end of chap. 7.
17. This disaffection to the world "soul" was quite widespread among young writers after World War I. Aldous Huxley expressed a similar repugnance in a conversation with Professor Louis Cazamian.

18. He used the word again, however, in his very last novel, *Islands in the Stream* (New York: Scribner, 1970), p. 100 and especially p. 191: "What he needs is to work well to save his soul. I don't know anything about souls. But he misplaced his the first time he went out to the Coast." He did not know what a soul was, but he did know that it could be saved or lost.

19. *Sartor Resartus,* Book I, chap. 3.

20. "A Clean Well-Lighted Place."

21. Ecclesiastes I: 2, 4-5. Thomas Wolfe, though belonging to a slightly younger generation, at times shared Hemingway's fundamental pessimism: "In everlasting terms—those of eternity—you and the Preacher may be right: for there is no greater wisdom than the wisdom of the *Ecclesiastes,* no acceptance finally so true as the acceptance of the rock. Man was born to live, to suffer, and to die, and what befalls him is a tragic lot. There is no denying this in the final end. But we must, dear Fox, deny it all along the way." Quoted by Maxwell Geismar in his introduction to the *Portable Thomas Wolfe* (New York: Viking, 1946), p. 25

22. *A Farewell to Arms,* chap. 25.

23. *Sartor Resartus,* Book I, chap. 7.

24. "Farewell the Separate Peace," in John K. M. McCaffery, op cit., p. 137.

25. Introduction to *Men at War,* p. 12.

26. *A Farewell to Arms,* chap. 35.

27. Ibid., chap. 32.

28. Ecclesiastes II: 24.

29. *A Farewell to Arms,* chap. 35.

30. Ecclesiastes III: 1, 3.

31. Robert Cohn is in a way a prefiguration of some of Saul Bellow's and Malamud's heroes. No wonder Bellow has in his turn rejected Hemingway and his code of WASP values.

32. Cf. this passage in *The Green Hills of Africa* (chap. 4), in which Hemingway discusses Tolstoy's early novel, *Sevastopol:* "It was a very young book and had one fine description in it, when the French take the redoubt and I thought about Tolstoy and what a great advantage an experience of war was to a writer. It was one of the major subjects and certainly one of the hardest to write truly of and those writers who had not seen it were always very jealous and tried to make it seem unimportant, or abnormal, or a disease as a subject, while, really, it was just something quite irreplaceable that they had missed."

33. Pascal, *Pensées* (Léon Brunschvicg ed., no. 347): "L'homme n'est qu'un roseau pensant, le plus faible de la nature . . . mais quand l'univers l'écraserait, l'homme serait encore plus noble que ce qui le tue, parce qu'il sait qu'il meurt et l'avantage que l'univers a sur lui, l'univers n'en sait rien."

34. Last page but one of *The Sun Also Rises.*

35. Ibid., chap. 14.

36. *Death in the Afternoon.*

37. *Green Hills of Africa,* chap. 5.

38. *Death in the Afternoon,* last page.

39. *To Have and Have Not,* chap. 15.
40. *For Whom the Bell Tolls,* chap. 18.
41. Ibid., chap. 13.
42. Ibid., chap. 36.
43. Ibid., chap. 13. The italics are mine.
44. Cf. *Islands in the Stream:* ". . . he was still in love with the first woman he had been in love with" (p. 8).
45. *Sartor Resartus,* Book II, chap. IX.
46. Ibid.
47. *Green Hills of Africa,* Part I, chap. 1.
48. Pascal, though a good Christian, feared nada as much as Hemingway and confessed that "le silence éternel des espaces infinis" (the eternal silence of infinite space) inspired him with awe. *(Pensées,* Léon Brunschvicg, ed., thoughts no. 205, 206).
49. The theme of universal love is taken up again in *Islands in the Stream,* when David, Thomas Hudson's youngest son, like Santiago, catches a big fish and fights with him just as epically. Hemingway makes him say afterward: "In the worst parts, when I was the tiredest I couldn't tell which was him and which was me. . . . Then I began to love him more than anything on earth. . . . I loved him so much when I saw him coming up that I couldn't stand it" (pp. 142-43).

11.

The Tragic
Transcendentalism of
Tennessee Williams

The same powerful current of desire flows through *A Streetcar Named Desire* as through *Desire Under the Elms.* In both plays, although invisible, it is nonetheless the titular hero and it carries away all the *dramatis personae* like straws. What Tennessee Williams offers us under this title is thus less a slice of Southern life than a mystery play in disguise—a projection of his *Weltanschauung* showing Man and Woman against a cosmic backdrop on which Light and Darkness, Good and Evil wage a perpetual war.

A Streetcar Named Desire indeed illustrates a certain Christian, and even Pascalian, conception of the human condition. It shows man constantly oscillating between two poles, partaking of the nature of angels through his soul and of that of beasts through his body, and thus being a confused mixture of the two, quite unable ever to be one to the exclusion of the other. Man is neither an angel nor a beast. Whoever denies this duality will be punished for it. "Qui veut faire l'ange, fait la bête." [1] The story of Blanche proves it. As she tells Mitch in scene VI, she married when she was still a very young girl and was only sixteen when she made the discovery of love. It was a blinding spiritual illumination rather than a physical experience: "It was like you suddenly turned on something that had always been half in shadow. . . ." Her young Adonis-like husband seemed equally pure, but he was actually torn between his heterosexual love for Blanche and his homosexual love for an old lover. When she found it out, she experienced a violent revulsion. Her angelic nature felt only disgust for the beast whose existence she did not suspect in her apparently angelic husband. She completely rejected the beastly side of human nature, but she was later punished for this unnatural sin, for she had henceforward to yield unconditionally to the demands of her own body. She became promiscuous: ". . . the searchlight which had been turned on the world was turned off again." [2] From then on she had to live in the darkness of her own body, to ask for anyone's help to fill up the void she felt inside. She became the slave of sex, because she had denied it.

Stella, on the contrary, though originally a star among stars, as her name indicates, and an angel among angels, has fully accepted her dual nature and consequently knows peace and fulfilment.

As to Stanley (Stanley the stud), he is closer to beasts than to angels, if we are to believe Blanche's description of him in scene IV, despite some redeeming features like his loyalty to Mitch, his comrade-in-arms, and his tenderness for Stella.

The most remarkable thing about this picture of the human condition is that it should be colored by the Christian notion of sin, but we must bear in mind that Tennessee Williams spent his childhood in the house of an Episcopalian clergyman, the Reverend Walter E. Dakin, his grandfather. He acknowledges himself that there was a puritan as well as a cavalier strain in his personality. He seems in particular to have always had a very strong sense of guilt. In his Foreword to *Sweet Bird of Youth,* he writes: "Guilt is universal. I mean a strong sense of guilt." [3] He attributes this in "Desire and the Black Masseur" (Desire again!) to a sense of incompletion or imperfection which we possess precisely because we also possess a sense of perfection, a belief in the absolute: "[Man] feels a part of himself to be like a missing wall or a room left unfurnished and he tries as well as he can to make up for it. The use of imagination, resorting to dreams or the loftier purpose of art, is a mask he devises to cover his incompletion." [4]

Now Blanche—that is to say himself, for "Blanche c'est moi," [5] believes in the existence of the absolute—like Antigone, though less stridently and though, unlike Antigone, she has been betrayed by her body and a sensuality which she cannot control, for, unfortunately, according to Tennessee Williams, man, that incomplete and imperfect creature, torn by the conflicting demands of his ambiguous nature, is not really free to choose his course. His fate is largely determined by the physiology he has inherited and by his environment, that is to say by social forces which exert upon him pressures which he cannot resist. In an interview which he gave to the *New York Herald Tribune,* Tennessee Williams declared: "I don't believe in 'original sin' [i.e., in predestination]. I don't believe in [born] villains and heroes,—only in right and wrong ways that individuals have taken, not by choice, but by necessity, or by still uncomprehended influences in themselves, their circumstances and their antecedents." [6] In "The Siege," he repeated the same thing in the form of an image:

> Sometimes I feel the island of myself . . .
> revolving frantic mirrors in itself
> beneath the pressure of a million thumbs.[7]

Man's fate is thus inescapable and his life a constant fall. In the poem entitled "Orpheus Descending," Tennessee Williams warns us:

> for you must learn, even you, what we have learned,
> the passion there is for declivity in this world,
> the impulse to fall that follows a rising fountain.[8]

Our birth is the beginning of our fall. In *Camino Real,* the Gypsy asks Kilroy the date of his birth in the following way: "Date of birth and place of that disaster?" and she later adds: "Baby, your luck ran out the day you were born." [9]

In this respect, Tennessee Williams fully shares the pessimism of Christianity as regards life here below and, like the romantics, he is especially obsessed by the flight of time. For him Time is our worst enemy: it is the instrument of Fate and the medium of our powerlessness. It ruthlessly drags us to our death: "[The time of our life] is short and it doesn't return again. It is slipping away while I write this, and while you read it, and the monosyllable of the clock is Loss, Loss, Loss, unless you devote your heart to its opposition." [10] (That is, to desire, which is the reverse of death.)

The most tragic problem man has to face is indeed the fact of death. Tennessee Williams himself has declared that *A Streetcar Named Desire* was "saturated with death," and Blanche in one of her speeches in scene I describes "the Dance of Death" at Belle Reve. The "grim Reaper" sooner or later mows down everyone—and this retrospectively—if one does not believe in the immortality of the soul and a system of rewards and punishments in the hereaf-ter—makes life here below meaningless and absurd and the world chaotic and broken, as in Hart Crane's poem, "The Broken Tower," quoted as an epigraph to *A Streetcar Named Desire*. This is precisely the discovery that Sebastian Venable makes in *Suddenly Last Summer*. Unlike Saint Sebastian, his namesake, Sebastian Ven-able (the opposite of Venerable) does not believe in a Christian God's plan and becomes totally demoralized when confronted with the mass slaughter of the newly hatched tortoises in the Galápagos. But, though Thanatos threatens all the characters in *A Streetcar Named Desire* and nearly gets Blanche, though the old Mexican vendor of "flores para los muertos" is always there in the wings, Death does not quite carry the day, for, as Tennessee Williams points out, Desire is the opposite of Death. Eros, to a large extent, neutralizes Thanatos, the merchant of red-hot tamales counteracts the old flower woman, and Desire rather than Death dominates the play. The Dance of Death at Belle Reve is a thing of the past. What we see on the stage is the Dance of Desire, in particular at the beginning of scene V, when Steve chasing his wife is almost metamorphosed into a faun or a satyr.

At this point, we encounter the fundamental ambiguity of Ten-nessee Williams's philosophy. Though an idealist, he believes in sexual desire as a force which transcends the individual. D. H. Lawrence was his master in this respect, and that is why he has dedicated *I Rise in Flames, Cried the Phoenix* to his memory. For him as for Lawrence, desire intensifies the vital urge which is in us and sets us on fire, as it were. Otherwise, the divine spark that is in us remains dormant and eventually dies out. In the Preface to *I Rise in Flames,* he wrote: "Lawrence felt the mystery and power of sex, as the primal life urge, and was the lifelong adversary of those who wanted to keep the subject locked in the cellars of prudery." In the play itself, he had Frieda Lawrence exclaim: "The meaning of Lawrence escapes you. In all his work he celebrates the body." [11]

So, though in *A Streetcar Named Desire* he seems to be deeply in sympathy with Blanche, and her nostalgic craving for innocence and purity, he is also on the side of Stanley and Stella and occasionally celebrates *machismo* and carnal love in lyrical terms to the sincere horror of Blanche. Side by side with his romantic idealism, there is in *A Streetcar Named Desire* a Lawrentian vitalism and an exaltation of sexual desire, which he defined in *Hard Candy* as "the fierceness and fire of the will of life to transcend the single body."[12] He even sang sexual desire in a play in verse characteristically entitled "The Purification":

Resistless it was
this coming of birds together
in heaven's center . . .
Plumage—song—the dizzy spiral of flight
all suddenly forced together
in one brief burning conjunction!
Oh—oh!
a passionate little spasm of wings and throats
that clutched—and uttered—darkness . . .
Down
  down
    down
Afterwards, shattered
we found our bodies in grass.[13]

This reads almost like Whitman's poem on "The Dalliance of the Eagles."

Tennessee Williams thus had a foot in both camps. His negative capability is not only dramatic—an inability to choose between Blanche and Stella or Blanche and Stanley—it is also philosophical—an inability to choose between the body and the soul, between materialism and spiritualism. It is even a religious form of negative capability. He cannot choose between God and the Devil.[14] In his eyes, the main thing is the impulse, the urge, the "élan vital," and he used Bergson's phrase at least once in his *Memoirs* (p. 101).

In practice, however, the dichotomy body-soul is usually toned down in his plays, because he tends to idealize sexual desire and add an element of tenderness to sexual lust. In an interview, he said: "I don't think there can be truly satisfactory sex without love." [15] In other words, he believes in the equation: lust + tenderness = love, which applies even to Stanley. Through love, it becomes possible to resist the propensity to declivity which is inherent in matter, and the physical world, which would otherwise look chaotic and broken, ceases to be meaningless. To return to Hart Crane's epigraph, there floats over Tennessee Williams's world "the visionary company of love."

Yet, this is only half-reassuring, for there is no certainty we can cling to, and Tennessee Williams's belief in God and the soul remains extremely vague and undogmatic, though he was brought up in the Episcopal church and his younger brother Dakin even obtained his conversion to Catholicism during one of his serious illnesses, when everyone thought he was going to die. "It did me no harm," Tennessee Williams afterward said, "I've always been very religious . . . and am still religious as a Catholic, although I do not subscribe to a great many of the things you are supposed to subscribe to, like the belief in individual immortality. . . . I love the poetry of the Church. And I love to receive communion." [16]

His characters, like himself, feel lonely and walled in in their ego. They try desperately to communicate, through the flesh if necessary, with the spiritual presence which they feel outside themselves, God present in others. But they succeed only intermittently. As Blanche says: "Sometimes there's God—so quickly!" [17] Whereas for Sartre, "l'enfer, c'est les autres," for Tennessee Williams hell is yourself, "when you ignore other people completely, that is hell," since, as Marlowe's Faustus had already found out, hell is where God is not. Only through a reciprocal dependency, that is to say only through love, can a person escape that solipsistic obsession with self which is the equivalent of hell, and thus find the equivalent of heaven.

All this makes up a rather dark and tragic vision of Man's position in a universe where he is condemned to grope for his way without ever finding certainty. And yet, as Don Quixote notes in *Camino Real:* "Life is an unanswered question, but let's still believe in the dignity and importance of the question." [18] Though terrible, life is, indeed, a wonderful and unfathomable mystery. Its force is irresistible. The violets in the mountains break the rocks, Tennessee Williams points out. [19] So he reveres life in all its forms. He respects it in particular in the very characters he creates. Though he intensifies and enlarges them, he does not try to explain them. Their ultimate motives remain undecipherable hieroglyphics. Why did Stanley treat Blanche so cruelly? Was he waging a war of aggression on her or was he only on the defensive? What was the true nature of Blanche? Was she fundamentally pure or impure? a saint or a whore? We shall never know. There will always be "something unspoken." [20]

> something unspoken
> . . .
> something that's delicate
> and dim and rare
> breathes in the space between
> a bed and a chair. [21]

Tennessee Williams insisted that his characters "must have that quality of life which is 'shadowy,' " and he added:

> Frankly I don't want people to leave the theatre . . . knowing everything about the characters they have witnessed that night in violent interplay. . . . Every moment of human existence is alive with uncertainty. . . . I want them [the spectators] to leave . . . feeling that they have met with a vividly allusive as well as disturbingly elusive fragment of human experience, one that not only points at truth, but at the *mysteries* of it [italics mine], much as they will leave this world, when they leave it, still wondering somewhat about what happened to them, and for what reason or purpose. [22]

One of the "mysteries" of his characters is their belief in the existence of an ideal which is nowhere to be found here below, and yet, even those who wallow in sex and filth cannot help despising the *hic et nunc,* the here and now. They prefer the infinity of dreams to the finite material world to which their bodies are confined. Thus Blanche escapes in her fantasies from the sordid world of Elysian Fields and takes refuge in the Belle Reve (of the symptomatic name) of her youth in an almost legendary and antebellum South where all women are beautiful and pure and all men perfect gentlemen. She spontaneously identifies herself with that late romantic heroine, Marguerite Gautier, *la Dame aux Camélias,*[23] and moves in a platonic world of pure essences: Beauty, Goodness, Truth, where everything is either white or blue, the blue of a child's eyes, of a cloudless sky, of the Holy Virgin's mantle in a Della Robbia picture, the blue—in her last speech—of her first lover's eyes.[24]

Not only are most of Tennessee Williams's heroes and heroines idealists at heart, but they are all marvellously articulate—like their creator. To a greater or lesser degree, they all speak like poets (in prose). Each of them, as it were, plays on his own "tinny piano with the infatuated fluency" of his more or less "dirty fingers," thus expressing "the spirit of the life which goes on" around him or her, to take up Tennessee Williams's very words in the stage directions for the opening scene of *A Streetcar Named Desire.* Blanche in particular again and again opens up vistas on the infinity of space and time far beyond the narrow limits of the claustrophobic apartment to which she is physically confined. In her own words, she turns an hour in New Orleans into "a little piece of eternity dropped into [our] hands." [25]

Moreover, a constant musical accompaniment (of noises as well as music proper) broadens the scenes of the play as they unfold before our eyes and helps give them cosmic dimensions. It suggests now sheer animal joy, now, on the contrary, nostalgic sadness. The noise made by the trains emphasizes the ruthless violence of Stanley. The screeches of the cats outside express the wildness of sexual desire, and Stanley echoes them when he caterwauls like a tomcat under Stella's window, after she has taken refuge with their neighbors upstairs. And, as the play progresses, these screeches become more and more insistent and threatening, like cries in the jungle, recalling the primal struggle for life of which every human action is but a part.

In short, Tennessee Williams's theater brings us face to face with "the impenetrable mystery which hides (and hides through absolute transparency) the mental nature." [26] We watch in awe his transcription in human terms of "the whole circle of animal life— tooth against tooth— . . . a yelp of pain and a grunt of triumph, until, at last, the whole menagerie, [not merely the glass menagerie], the whole chemical mass is mellowed and refined for higher use." [27] For all the tragic dichotomies which divide his world, for all his uncertainties, we cannot but believe him when he declares with some embarrassment to the *Partisan Review* interviewer that he was "a lover of God and a believer." [28] This faith, however shaky and problematic it may appear, rests on a vivid perception of life as a transcendent reality and turns the world into a thing of beauty and mystery, and makes it a source of perpetual awe and wonder.

Notes

1. Blaise Pascal, *Pensées*, no. 358, in *Pensées*, Léon Brunschvicg, ed.
2. *A Streetcar Named Desire*, end of scene VI, p. 96 in Signet Edition.
3. *Sweet Bird of Youth* (London: Secker & Warburg, 1959), p. 9.
4. *One Arm and Other Stories* (Norfolk, Conn.: New Directions, 1954), p. 85.
5. "I can identify completely with Blanche," he said to the *Playboy* interviewer, "we are both hysterics." *Playboy* (April 1973), p. 72C.
6. *New York Herald Tribune*, March 3, 1957.
7. *In the Winter of Cities* (Norfolk, Conn.: New Directions, 1952), p. 20.
8. Ibid., p. 28.
9. *Camino Real* (Norfolk, Conn.: New Directions, 1953), pp. 111, 115.
10. *A Streetcar Named Desire*, end of Introduction, op. cit. (p. 10).
11. *I Rise in Flames, Cried the Phoenix* (Norfolk, Conn.: New Directions, 1951).
12. "A Violin Case and a Coffin," *Hard Candy* (Norfolk, Conn.: New Directions, 1954), p. 97.
13. *Twenty-Seven Wagons Full of Cotton, and Other One-Act Plays* (Norfolk, Conn.: New Directions, 1946), p. 45.
14. His inclination for the Devil appears in particular in *Where I Live*, where he quotes approvingly this sentence by Strindberg: "They call it love-hatred, and it hails from the pit" (p. 73). Emerson himself, after all, reacted in much the same way, because in "Self-Reliance" he went so far as to answer: ". . . if I am the Devil's child, I will live then from the Devil" to a friend who objected: "But these impulses may be from below, not from above."
15. *Playboy*, op. cit., p. 74C.
16. Ibid., p. 84AB.
17. Last words of scene VI, op cit., p. 96.
18. *Camino Real*, op. cit., p. 159.

19. Ibid., p. 161.
20. This is the title of one of the plays in *Twenty-Seven Wagons Full of Cotton.*
21. *In the Winter of Cities,* op. cit., p. 104.
22. *Where I Live: Selected Essays* (Norfolk, Conn.: New Directions, 1978), pp. 72-74.
23. *A Streetcar Named Desire,* scene VI, op. cit., p. 88.
24. Ibid., scene XI, p. 136.
25. Ibid., scene V, p. 83.
26. Ralph Waldo Emerson, *Natural History of the Intellect* (Boston: Houghton Mifflin, 1893), p. 5.
27. *The Conduct of Life,* "Fate" (London: Macmillan, 1892), p. 29.
28. Cecil Brown, "Interview with Tennessee Williams," *Partisan Review,* vol. 45, no. 2, p. 296.

12.

A Neglected
Transcendentalist Poet of
the Twentieth Century:
Walter Lowenfels (1897-1976)

Arma virumque cano.

Walter Lowenfels's name does not appear in the *Literary History of
the United States* or the *Oxford Companion to American Literature.* Sylvia
Beach and Janet Flanner both ignore him in their books of reminiscences. George Wickes in his *Americans in Paris, 1903-1939,* men-
tions him twice in passing and rather condescendingly. He is the
most neglected American poet of the twentieth century, and yet he
shared a prize with E. E. Cummings in 1930 and Henry Miller
considered him "probably *the* poet of the age," [1] and made him the
hero of a chapter of *Black Spring.* He depicted him there under the
name Jabberwhorl Cronstadt, a poet of Eastern European Jewish
origin endowed with a prodigious verbal skill, capable of giving
sense to the nonsense of Lewis Carroll's jabberwocky, a whirl of
words, singing Alpha and Omega, singing hallelujah.[2] The only
American critic who ever paid any attention to Lowenfels was
Kenneth Rexroth. He devoted a page to him in his essay on "The
influence of French poetry on American." [3] This is strictly all. He
undoubtedly deserves to be better known, for he was the closest
approximation to Walt Whitman in the twentieth century, singing
like him both the infinity of the cosmos and the greatness of Democracy, "life immense" and "Modern Man en-masse."

163

Though he was born in New York in 1897 (in May like Whitman), he could not have said like him: "born of parents born here from parents the same and their parents the same," [4] for his parents were Jewish immigrants from Eastern Europe and his father, far from being a failure like Whitman's father, was a successful businessman, a prosperous wholesale dealer in butter, who, in the poet's own words, "had made enough money to bring him up as a well-fed child and a healthy man." So Walter Lowenfels, behaving like a dutiful son, learned "how to buy and sell butter" and became quite adept at doing it, but in 1926, at twenty-nine years of age, he suddenly decided to break with this meaningless routine. It was the end of his "first life," as he said. He left "the social security of butter for the hazards of Paris and poetry." [5] Although he had not taken part in World War I, he had been badly shaken by it and can be considered a virtual member of the lost generation. Like Hemingway and T. S. Eliot, he felt surrounded by death on all sides in the middle of a dying civilization, in a godless world. In Paris, his friend Michael Fraenkel, the author of a romance very aptly entitled *Werther's Younger Brother* (1930), introduced him (and Henry Miller) to the works of Spengler and Nietzsche,[6] and he absorbed their pessimism and reveled in the thought of death. In his eyes, there was only one possibility of salvation: through artistic creation. So he spent all his time with Fraenkel, Anaïs Nin, and Henry Miller (who found him too intellectual, "all mind, all ideas") [7], talking endlessly about death—and love—or writing poems. He published some of them in Eugène Jolas's *Transition* and others in the form of pamphlets or booklets. But, since he regarded the world as "washed up," "the only thing that one could do was write elegies." [8] Consequently, he began a book entitled *Some Deaths,* consisting of a series of elegies and winding up with one called "The Suicide." A draft of this book was published in 1934. *Steel 1937,* though published in the United States after his return here, belongs to this first period and marked the end of his Paris years. It was a collection of poems about the Spanish Civil war and the CIO drive to organize Little Steel, in which he tried to carry on the technical discoveries he had made in Paris and to apply them to new subjects.[9] For his stay in Paris could not last indefinitely. He was married and had three daughters. War was threatening in

Europe. Like many of his fellow expatriates, he was obliged to go home and work for a living. He did so in 1934 after burning all his unused manuscripts as Henry Miller, who was witness to this holocaust, has described it in *The Air-Conditioned Nightmare.*[10] He felt it was the end of his career and he was dead as a poet.[11]

So he returned to the United States and once more bought and sold butter "from 9 AM to 5 PM, writing poetry in his non-butter time." [12] But after two years, he again broke with the world of business, this time because he had heard the call of politics and become keenly interested in the working-class movement. He was forty by then, but "went through a new youth and adolescence." He joined the Communist Party and from 1940 to 1954 was reporter for and later editor of the Philadelphia edition of the *Daily Worker.* His political activities led to his arrest by the FBI in 1953, during the McCarthy era. He was jailed and tried. He was charged with teaching and abetting the violent overthrow of the United States government, and sentenced to two years' imprisonment. He never served this sentence, for it was quashed by a higher court for lack of evidence.

After he retired from active service in his sixties, he was busier than ever as a writer, turning all his experiences into poetry. This last phase of his career was probably the most fruitful. Actually he had returned to poetry as early as 1951. "I was about 54, he said, [when I] resumed writing poems as a major occupation. A turning-point was the death of a seven-year-old girl I knew. I didn't go to the funeral. I wrote a poem." [13] "Within a day or two of my Great Decision [to write poems again], he added, I got a new insight into Whitman," [13] and from then on, he "de-practicalized" himself, to use his own word. He ceased to care for practical matters and decided "to be practical on a higher level, a more creative level," which did not mean "unpoliticizing" himself, it meant, on the contrary, being "political on a higher level," "relating ideas and deeds, poems and politics." [14] He was particularly affected by the atom bomb. "In 1945, he wrote, we put our hands in the mechanism of the universe and none of us have ever been the same." So he wrote poems "to exorcise the evil, the terror that surrounds us." [15] "Not that every poem is a poem about peace and war." On the contrary, "every poem is a love poem." [16]

Though living in a lonely cottage in the middle of the barren pineland of Peekskill, some thirty-five miles from New York City, his birthplace, he never ceased to feel directly concerned by what was going on in the world at large until his death in 1976. As he pointed out himself, there was, however, a considerable difference between the two poetical periods of his career. Whereas in the 1920s and 1930s, as an avant garde poet he was writing "for an audience of no one," in the latter, in the 1950s and 1960s, like the great Mexican fresco painters whom he admired (Orozco, Siqueiros, Rivera), he was "trying to speak the language of everyone asking only to live." [17]

Despite his political commitment and his desire to be the poet of the people, Walter Lowenfels was fundamentally, like Whitman, a transcendentalist writer for whom the physical world was an ever-baffling mystery, an undecipherable message in coded language, a deceptive appearance hiding an unfathomable reality, and he considered it his duty to go beyond this appearance. He moved

> among the centuries
> of how many fathoms—forgotten spring.[18]

Beyond reality (in the delusory everyday meaning of the word), he reached what he called "Reality Prime":

> What we are after is Reality Prime. That is where you climb up the audience ladder and throw it away. Then you arrive at a point where your poet transcends the class limits of his vision, leaps out of the lenses of his eyes and sees more than he knows.[19]

For "the artist is a master of revelations" [20] and, for his part, Walter Lowenfels was "not interested in explanation but revelation." [21] There is, as it were, an "underground river of existence which he was able to tap now and then." [22]

Like Whitman, he was not contained between his hat and boots. He transcended the limits of his body and traveled through the cosmos at the speed of light. He had an extraordinarily vivid sense of the infinity of space and time which never left him and which he tried to communicate in the language of modern physics, frequently quoting Einstein's theorem: $E = mc^2$.[23]

> We are the should-be's of collapsed supernovae
> doomed to winter it among galactic halos
> in the cool universe of undisturbed suns.
> There is no pain
>   only
> a swift wind of hydrogen
> sweeps us
> through centuries of magnetic storms . . .
> We are the diffuse gas of electronic
>   degeneracy
> cast in cosmic particles in the flesh . . .
> It took me six billion years
> to get just that distance from the sun
>   I need to breathe
> and just near enough my oxygen supply
>   to stay alive.[24]

He is the poet of the space age and invites us to "a guided tour of the solar system." [25] He believes "we are on the verge of intergalactic communication with other living presences many staryears away." [26] No wonder Robert Gover calls him "Walter the Cosmic Ad Agency copywriter making advertisements for the more mysterious aspects of human existence." [27]

Two sciences help him in his exploration of the cosmos: geology and astronomy, which also fascinated Whitman. The former reminds him that man is a new arrival on earth and will some day become an extinct species in his turn, since we live in "the Third Inter-Glacial Era" which will not last for ever.[28] It thus helps him to make tangible to us the transiency of our existence as opposed to the endlessness of time. As to the latter, it feeds his imagination with fantastic facts and figures and makes him realize the infinity of space. We are thus, in his vision, very provisionally suspended over the void of Einstein's space-time continuum:

> As we sat that hour at that café on that
>   boulevard
> Before our accidental angle crashes
>   down the space abyss
> Of time's perpetual catastrophe.[29]

His poems often confront us with a rather frightening "inhuman, geological and astronomical universe." [30] This dehumanization of the cosmos, however, does not frighten him, for he has two methods of avoiding fear and despair—the same as Whitman's: humor and lyricism (which in a way are twins—antipodean twins, if I may say so).

The vision of an infinite universe in which man appears as a negligible particle sometimes seems to him "a cosmic joke," [31] and fills him with exultation and exaltation. One of his poems (in prose) quite literally becomes a tall story and gives a new version of Genesis with Paul Bunyan in the role of God:

> Paul Bunyan . . . nursed on the waters of Lake Superior, and when he drank the big lake dry, he started screaming for more. That blew up a range of mountains on the north shore . . . etc. etc.[32]

It is all a "scientific vaudeville . . . called The World as Good Fun," and "the real gasser" comes "when some

> Pentagonian computer
> thought it was the spiral nebula in Andromeda attacking us
> and the last smile of the last child went into orbit
>   and cried silently forever after.[33]

(Savagery and civilization being relative notions, Pentagonians are the Patagonians of the twentieth century.)

One of his most successful poems in this vein is "For an Unsuccessful Suicide" (in *Found Poems and Others*). When in this mood, he can make fun even of death:

> Consider the traffic jam
>   if death didn't help rid us
>   of these monsters—our dead selves.[34]

In his poems, life becomes a game in which real and ideal become interchangeable, and he juggles with them.

But he can reverse the sense of his juggling and then humor turns into lyricism. Everything becomes a source of wonder rather than laughter. Everything is a miracle:

> Every cubic inch of space
> Is a miracle including
> Cosmic spherules and meteoric dust
> electronic trajectories
> fluid mechanics. . . .[35]

Everything that lives fills him with surprise and admiration and the world becomes one vast continuum of perpetually renewed life with which he communes continually:

> There are in me such tales of flowers and change
> of occupation of breathing things
> of absorption centrally
> I have to look but an instant
> to sponge-in living things.[36]

("To sponge-in" is here the equivalent of Whitman's favorite verb "to absorb.")

He then feels perfectly at home in the universe and can exclaim with Apollinaire:

> the world is enough
> and that is enough.[37]

And this explains how he could sympathize with the philosophical pantheism of Giordano Bruno:

> This giant order of huge starry beings
> hurtling their kisses into freezing voids
> are not in love with our small human things;
> but he loved them and sought their human laws.[38]

His cosmic vision led him to define "the essence of the poem" in the following terms:

> to catch that millionth of a microsecond that crosses the gap between the yesterday and the tomorrow people—to language this incredible speed that's whirling us towards the hydrogen storms of outer space, and pit it on the wall of here and now, so that we live in a sort of forever, an instant frozen in words. . . .[39]

In other words, a poem must suggest the infinite context surrounding the least object. Or, as he also said, a poet constantly attempts to answer the question: what time is it?—that is to say, where am I in the cosmos? Let me get my bearings. That is why he described himself as trying "to report human experience at any particular instant within the country I inhabit, but with the consciousness of the rest of the world" [40]—which is quite close to what Wordsworth meant when he said in *The Prelude* that he described "parts as parts, but with the feeling of the whole." And this corresponds exactly also to Coleridge's definition of imagination as "an esemplastic power," shaping all things into one.[41]

But there is an outrage and a scandal in this wonderful world—though Walter Lowenfels never uses such words—and that is death, which, from the very start, as we have seen, obsessed and shocked him. Why do all things have to die sooner or later, from stars to spores, from men to rocks? He shared his friend Fraenkel's pessimism in this respect:

> I see death then as something not to be conquered or done away with, but an ever-present enemy to know, and whose

grip may be avoided for a while by the dance of poetry, the nexus of love, the transformation of religion, the revolution of society, but death . . . can never cease existing in a world in which life must feed on life and energy is continually being consumed. . . .[42]

He protested because human life was so short:

A copper coin or a stone
outlives any of us.[43]

This situation is all the more absurd because "poems are one evidence that we know how to be more than rocks. Our whole history is a living protest against geology." [44] So there were times when he was in revolt against the human condition itself, against God (but he hardly ever used the word, for he generally considered God a useless "deus ex machina") [45]: "it's not just tyrants or oppression that poets oppose . . . they are against the universe, and in their most powerful and passionate outbursts at the human condition [i.e., at death], they are at the same time affirming the unique and precious instant that we breathe and live." [46] In short, for all his existentialist disgust with the absurdity of the human lot, he clung to life as it is. Though he celebrated with sympathy and emotion the suicide of a poet who drowned himself (Hart Crane), developing in his honor Ariel's song on the supposed death of Miranda's father ("Full fathom five . . ."), he was "anti-suicide" himself [48] and protested against the romantic apology for suicide among writers: "It's true that a number of writers have killed themselves, been murdered, or gone nuts. What matters is not how they died, but what they wrote." [49] In short, he was in love with life and perfectly satisfied with "just the comma of being here / among milk bottles and constellations / in love with our parenthesis of passage between Andromeda and Peekskill. . . ." [50] ". . . if I leave a sad word behind, do I have to tell you it's a forgery?" he wrote at the end of one of his collections of poems.[51] He loved change, regarded a static instant not as heaven, but as hell,[52] and conceived God (when he mentioned him at all) as synonymous with perpetual Protean change: "You didn't know I believe in god [without a capital]? Of course I do and not just one god, or just once. He just can't keep from exploding not once or twice, but all the time, dying too in the same way that everything gets born—in fact you can't tell the difference, it's all simultaneous—as Barnum said, the greatest show on earth." [53]

Yet (I cannot avoid this seesawing which is his, not mine), he never got completely reconciled with the scandal of death. To take up the metaphor of his "Epitaph for my punctuation," though he loved the mere comma of his ephemeral being and the simple parenthesis of his life, he could not help regretting that it should be followed by points of suspension and a final mark of interrogation. He wondered what would become of that precious self of his, the sum total of all the experiences he had so carefully and voluptuously "sponged-in" during his stay in this world. Though, unlike Whitman, he never sang his Self or used the word "soul," [54] which had become almost obsolete in literature between the two wars, he could not avoid a certain anxiety at times.

But he had a powerful antidote at his disposal, since he was not only the poet of the cosmos, but also the poet of democracy. Company and comradeship enabled him to forget death. In fact, he considered loneliness the only true form of death: "Death is when you have no more friends left and nobody says hello." [55] Like Whitman he was the singer of "the love of comrades." His ideal democracy was essentially characterized by equality and fraternity. Though he translated Paul Eluard's poem on liberty,[56] he never sang it himself. He dreamed of a society in which all men would love each other, in which, as opposed to the present one, "man uneats man." [57] He shared Rousseau's delusion that man is born good—and so believed that if the greed of capitalism were removed and society organized along socialistic lines, the world would become the best of all possible worlds. He considered it therefore his duty to sing love in order to prepare the coming of this idyllic society, and he wrote a poem entitled: "Every poem is a love poem," [58] and proclaimed in another poem (lovingly translated from a South American poet):

> My heart has become a lover
> going out to meet the world.

Poetry is a tower lighting up what is real—
a song that says *yes*
to all mankind.[59]

And he added, in conclusion to "a poem written after an editorial
board meeting":

    In conclusion, Comrades Editors,
    A poem is a forget-me-not in a button-hole that never closes.
    A poem should be about nothing and so full of love
    you don't even have to mention the word—
    just a whisper bringing down manna from the heavens
    softening the desert stones and arroyos . . .[60]

"As our Amerindian ancestors put it," he also said,

    What is more beautiful
    than the land that has no grave
    because there is no fear . . .
    because the light of wisdom
    is everywhere . . .

    and love
    LOVE
    LOVE   [crescendo]
    (also more love)
    dividing the sun
    putting ribbons on the storms
    turning each body into a flower
    looking America for you.[61]

He was thus holding the hand of the Beat poets of the sixties on
one side and the hand of Whitman on the other, for he dreamed of
a Passage to India of his own, "to more than India":

    O show us the road to the Indies
    lead us to that continent of our dreams.

However, his mythical India was not Whitman's "land of budding bibles," but the place

> where the workers are always right
> a poem is blooming in every oak
>   in Louisiana—[62]

(Another reminiscence of Whitman: "I Saw in Louisiana a Live-Oak Growing.")

Unfortunately we are still very far from that India of the poet's dream. The world is constantly at war, and since the first atom bomb was dropped on Hiroshima in 1945, the destruction of the whole human species at any minute has become possible:

> there are enough megatons in the world
> to kill everybody 12 times.[63]

We are all threatened by deadly atomic radiation:

> In South Jersey [where the poet lived]
> the wild laurel breathes over our tomato patches.
> A pine wind dusts our hands and faces.
> A farmer turns in his sleep wondering—
> will morning bring radium or rain? [64]

"We live each instant as if it were the last, at the edge of somebody's nuclear button." [65]

His friend Howard McCord objected to all this: "Man must love. Men can't love. It is that simple. Last century's death is a preview of this century's death." [66] But Lowenfels did not accept this Christian pessimism (McCord was a Catholic). His answer was that socialism could change the living conditions of people and could even change man; "the alternative is organization—to organize a different life. . . . The world as a poem [under socialism] or as death [under present conditions]. There is no in between." [67]

Because there is no in-between, it is the duty of the poet, according to Lowenfels, to commit himself. "The artist is the first politician." [68] Commitment has become all the more urgent, he claimed, because "we are all hung up on the hot line between atomic catastrophe and human triumph [through the universal victory of socialism]." [69] For his part, he did not hesitate. He discovered socialism in the late thirties and, when he was "born again as a poet" in the early fifties, he sang his political faith with a neophyte's zeal and fervor. Like his transcendentalist predecessors, he preached disobedience and called for revolt against the powers that be, "because things are as they are, not as they should be." He exhorted his newborn twelfth grandchild to resist and live in perpetual unrest:

> Don't stop the scream you got born with.
> Resist, resist, and then resist . . .
> . . . follow your smile-scream syndrome
> and you'll reach the Himalayas
> of eternal unrest.[70]

He went even further than Whitman's "resist much, obey little." He was and wanted to be an "untranquilizer." "All you will catch from me, he said, is high blood pressure." [71] For all contemporary problems kept worrying and outraging him and were so many occasions for passionate protests—especially racial problems. He was the eloquent champion of all ethnic minorities in the United States, from blacks to Indians and Chicanos and even Eskimos. He thus wrote a loving and angry poem on the killing of four black girls in the basement of a Sunday School in Birmingham ("The Execution"),[72] and in the poem entitled "At Bemidji Falls," he lamented the disappearance of the Indian hunters:

> The waterfall
> was there when you were asleep.
> Indians used to trap around the bend.
> Yes that's the wigwam your ancestor
> blew to hell for a dollar and a half.[73]

He identified with all oppressed minorities:

> I am not the North American you take me for—
>   writing poems in New York . . .

I am going to school with the campesinos and
  learning how to spell.
My skin has changed color, even in the dark
You can tell which side I am on.[74]

He wanted all forms of black culture to be recognized in the United States: music, dancing, even language (black English), and in order to make up for the lily-white quality and colorblindness of the *Oxford Book of American Verse* edited by F. O. Matthiessen (who was an advanced liberal, however),[75] he edited himself *Poets of Today: A New American Anthology,* which included a large number of black and Indian poets, and later, *In a Time of Revolution—Poems from Our Third World.* He thought American art must cease to be exclusively European and, on the contrary, "claim traditions in Asia, Africa, Latin-America . . . with a new emphasis on Indian, Labor, Jewish and Negro cultures in our own country." [76]

Many of his poems are thus stamped with political militancy—a political militancy too often inspired by a rather naïve and blind belief in the blackness of the Pentagon and the infallibility of socialism. He goes so far as to write, for instance, to his "imaginary daughter": "The revolution breaks the deadly cycle of repetition—the same snake swallowing the same tail," [77] as if "the deadly cycle of repetition" did not affect revolutions as well. His poetry too often verges on crude political propaganda, and that is one of its great weaknesses. He was fully aware of the danger, but claimed that he was "not a poet despite his political convictions: rather, it [was his] political convictions that [were] the final cement in [his] life-work as a poet." Besides, he said, "you can't divide a poet when he writes a poem from the same person when he does something 'political.' " [78] True, but there is a difference between being merely politically committed, as Emerson and Whitman were on certain occasions—not all the time—and belonging to a political party and being obliged to follow the party line.

So, though he claimed he was a poet *thanks to* his politics, I will rather contend that he was one *despite* them—because there were times when he forgot the existence of the atom bomb and all the other problems which usually beset him. He acknowledged it himself in a way when he wrote to a friend: "It's out of the impossibility of writing poems in our time that I have written some," [79] for, as he said, "we all feel and write about the usual things—spring, love, children, and just now, a red cardinal hopping across the grass looking for edibles, completely unaware of the Strontium 90 count." [80]

True, he also said: "Poems are incubating today not only in spring flowers and beautiful bodies, but in schools, the streets, wherever you find unrest and uprisings." [81] But, for all his socialism, he aimed above all at transcending reality and giving quasi-cosmic dimensions to the present sensation, necessarily limited in space and time, for a poem can "give us a momentary dilation of our vision," increase our awareness of "the enormous value of that instant of being alive." [82] He could obtain this by breaking all current poetical conventions and stereotypes, by "break[ing] out of the strait-jacket of literary texts," and by "transforming ordinary prose words into little flashes of lightning" [83] after wrenching them from their usual context. As we have seen, he also enlisted the sciences: geology, astronomy, and modern physics. His ideal was "to use the language of today for today's emotions." Consequently, he, like Whitman, felt it his duty to incorporate the latest discoveries of science and to use "the clean, new, scientific word woven into the fabric of the poem so quietly the reader doesn't sense anything, but the contemporary pulse modulation." "That's the test of language, he concluded, "that it is alive with today's electronics—not Ben Franklin's kite key." [84] His language undoubtedly passes this test, and he had every right to compose an "Elegy for the Old Language," as he did.[85] His poetry is, in his own words, a

Cosmic butterfly
spreading its wings
to absorb the eternal flow of solar energy.[86]

It was not a mere matter of technique, however, as he would like us to believe. If it had been, it would not have been poetry. We must also take into account the transmuting power of his imagination, which enabled him to turn "everything into something else"—a formula which he picked up from Mircea Eliade,[87] and which would not be a bad definition for surrealism. For his part, he proudly defined his poetry as "socialist surrealism," [88] a very apt phrase.

Such was the poet whom I regard as, in a way, the Whitman of the twentieth century. He does not have the same power, but, in spots, he too soars quite high. He was uneven and complex. His poetry ranges all the way from sheer political propaganda to inspired surrealism, from nature poetry to the celebration of modern industry. It is frequently either purely socialistic or wholly surrealistic. He did not always succeed in fusing the two into that "socialist surrealism" which he regarded as his aim. He may have been hampered by a certain *pudeur,* a certain modesty, an un-Whitmanesque reluctance to affirm the existence of the Spirit, though the Spirit definitely bloweth in his poetry. It was this *pudeur* which made him compare himself to "a pilot-fish" instead of calling himself a prophet like his master. Reading his works, we feel all the time that his ambition was to make human the inhuman universe in which we live.[89] In all circumstances, he boldly asserted his profound humanity, for he was at heart an irreducible individualist. As he said: "I don't agree with practically everybody. That's what drives me to poems." [90]

Notes

1. Quoted in the Introduction to Walter Lowenfels, *The Poetry of My Politics* (Homestead, Fla.: Olivant Press, 1963), p. 4.
2. Henry Miller, *Black Spring* (Paris: Obelisk Press, 1938).
3. Kenneth Rexroth, *Assays* (Norfolk, Conn.: New Directions, 1961), p. 167.
4. *Leaves of Grass,* "Song of Myself", sec. 1, 1.7.
5. See the Foreword (erroneously, but suggestively misprinted "Foreward") to *We Are All Poets Really* (Buffalo, N.Y.: Intrepid Press, 1968), p. 5.
6. *The Life of Fraenkel's Death* (in collaboration with Howard McCord) (Pullman, Washington: Washington State University Press, 1970), p. 6.
7. Anaïs Nin, *Diary,* vol. II (1936-1939) (New York: Harvest Books, 1967), p. 173.
8. See the Foreword to *We Are All Poets Really,* p. 5.
9. See Robert Gover, ed., *The Portable Walter Lowenfels* (New York: International Publishers, 1968), p. 16.
10. *The Air-Conditioned Nightmare* (London: Secker & Warburg, 1947), pp. 9-10.
11. *We Are All Poets Really,* p. 5.
12. Robert Gover, ed., *The Portable Walter Lowenfels,* (New York: International Publishers, 1969), p. 14.

13. *We Are All Poets Really,* p. 34.
14. Ibid., pp. 32-33.
15. Foreword to *Poets of Today* (New York: International Publishers, 1964), p. 5.
16. Prologue to *In a Time of Revolution, Poems from Our Third World,* ed. by Walter Lowenfels (New York: Random House, 1969), p. 7.
17. *Thou Shalt Not Overkill* (Belmont, Mass.: Hellric Publications, 1968), p. 1.
18. "Elegy for D. H. Lawrence," *We Are All Poets Really,* p. 24.
19. *Reality Prime* (Pages from a Journal) (Brooklyn, N.Y.: Cycle Press, 1974), p. 25.
20. *We Are All Poets Really,* p. 30.
21. *Reality Prime,* p. 18.
22. Ibid., p. 51.
23. For instance, in *Thou Shalt Not Overkill,* p. 6, "As if arriving."
24. "My Spectrum Analysis," ibid., p. 31, and also in *Translations from Scorpius* (Monmouth, Maine: Poetry Dimension Press, 1966), unpaged.
25. "Elegy for the old language," *Some Deaths* (Highlands, N.C.: Jonathan Williams, 1964), p. 4.
26. *Reality Prime,* p. 49.
27. *Portable Walter Lowenfels,* p. 128.
28. "As if arriving," *Thou Shalt Not Overkill,* p. 6.
29. "On the Impossibility of Meeting Hubert Juin," *Found Poems and Others* (New York: Barlenmir House, 1972), p. 38.
30. *Reality Prime,* p. 48.
31. *We Are All Poets Really,* p. 41.
32. "How It Started," *Translations from Scorpius.*
33. "My Spectrum Analysis," *Thou Shalt Not Overkill,* p. 32.
34. *To an Imaginary Daughter* (New York: Horizon Press, 1964), p. 10.
35. *Found Poems and Others,* p. 7.
36. "Elegy for D. H. Lawrence," *We Are All Poets Really,* p. 21.
37. "Apollinaire," *Some Deaths,* p. 50.
38. "Giordano Bruno," ibid., p. 56.
39. "Survival Kit," manuscript fragment which he sent to me, published in a slightly different form as the concluding poem in *Found Poems and Others.*
40. *We Are All Poets Really,* p. 64.
41. He was a great reader of Coleridge's *Biographia Literaria.* See *Portable Lowenfels,* p. 31.
42. *The Life of Fraenkel's Death,* p. 64.
43. "American Voices" (II), *Thou Shalt Not Overkill,* p. 44.
44. Letter to Jack Lindeman in *The Poetry of My Politics,* p. 69.
45. *The Life of Fraenkel's Death,* p. 57.
46. *The Writing on the Wall,* p. [4].
47. "The Suicide," *Land of Roseberries* (Mexico: el corno emplumado, 1965), p. 39.
48. "30 suicides in a glass case," *Found Poems and Others,* p. 39.
49. "For an Unsuccessful Suicide," *Some Deaths,* p. 83.
50. "Epitaph for my punctuation," *Found Poems and Others,* p. 52.

51. "I belong," last page of *Translations from Scorpius.*
52. *The Poetry of My Politics,* p. 87.
53. Letter to Bob Grover, *We Are Really All Poets,* p. 42. See also the conclusion of "Apollinaire," "where he writes in particular: "the world is constantly building / dying into beginning" *(Some Deaths,* p. 50).
54. See this passage in *The Life of Fraenkel's Death:* "When the distinction between the living and the non-living was great, when the 'soul' counted for something, then the urge to get the body from which the soul had departed away and out of sight . . . was logical. But now no soul, no distinction between the living and the dead, and so why bury?" (pp. 27-28).
55. *To an Imaginary Daughter,* p. 33. See also "The only death is to be alone," in "American Voices."
56. *Thou Shalt Not Overkill,* pp. 57-59.
57. *Reality Prime,* p. 19. This conceit, incidentally, is worthy of E. E. Cummings. There are others in his poems.
58. *Some Deaths,* p. 8.
59. "With Roots in Guatemala," ibid., p. 30.
60. "Magazine," ibid., p. 46.
61. *Thou Shalt Not Overkill,* p. 28.
62. "Magazine," *Some Deaths,* p. 45.
63. "My Spectrum Analysis," *Thou Shalt Not Overkill,* p. 33.
64. "American Voices" (II), ibid., p. 43.
65. *Thou Shalt Not Overkill,* p. 1.
66. *The Life of Fraenkel's Death,* p. 56.
67. Ibid., p. 57.
68. *We Are All Poets Really,* p. 30.
69. Introduction to *The Writing on the Wall,* p. [1].
70. *Found Poems and Others,* p. 35.
71. *We Are All Poets Really,* p. 36.
72. *Land of Roseberries,* pp. 12-13.
73. Ibid., pp. 11-12. See also "I am tired of fighting," from Chief Joseph's surrender speech in *Found Poems and Others,* p. 31.
74. "Island Paradise," *Some Deaths,* p. 67.
75. *The Poetry of My Politics,* pp. 15-22. See also Introduction to *The Writing on the Wall,* p. [3].
76. Ibid., p. 40.
77. *To an Imaginary Daughter,* p. 34.
78. *We Are All Poets Really,* p. 38.
79. Letter to Aaron Kurts in *Found Poems and Others,* p. 43.
80. See *supra,* n. 71.
81. *The Writing on the Wall,* p. [2].
82. *In A Time of Revolution,* p. [8].
83. *The Writing on the Wall,* p. [2].
84. *We Are All Poets Really,* p. 51. He never had any scientific training and picked

up what he knew of modern science from a popular magazine, *Scientific American*, which he frequently referred to.

85. *Some Deaths*, pp. 4-5.
86. *We Are All Poets Really*, p. 42.
87. Ibid., p. 30.
88. The phrase is actually McCord's in *The Life of Fraenkel's Death*, p. 36.
89. *Reality Prime*, p. 48.
90. *The Poetry of My Politics*, p. 72.

Index

Index of Walt Whitman's Poems Quoted and/or Discussed